Flash
for the REAL World

e-commerce case studies

Full/Queen New Hope

Rotate

Rotation: 330 °

Delete

Depth: 84 "

View

Width: 54 "

Height: 44 "

SAMS

201 West 103rd Street,
Indianapolis, Indiana 46290

Steve Street

Flash for the Real World:
E-Commerce Case Studies

ii

Copyright © 2002 by Sams Publishing

International Standard Book Number: 0-672-32079-7

Library of Congress Catalog Card Number: 00-108996

Printed in the United States of America

First Printing: July 2001

04   03   02   01   4   3   2   1

Trademarks

Warning and Disclaimer

Executive Editor
Jeff Schultz

Development Editor
Kate Small

Managing Editor
Charlotte Clapp

Project Editor
Elizabeth Finney

Copy Editor
Michael Henry

Indexer
Sandra Henselmeier

Sheila Schroeder

Mandie Frank

Proofreader
Plan-It Publishing

Team Coordinator
Amy Patton

Media Developer
Dan Scherf

Interior Designer
Dan Armstrong

Cover Designer
Evan Karatzas

Page Layout
Ayanna Lacey

Contents at a Glance

Table of Contents

About the Author

Steve Street has been creating interactive media since the early 1990s. He's developed unique and advanced solutions for a variety of clients including AT&T, Bose Corporation, IBM, Lotus Development Corporation, Prudential, Houghton Mifflin, and many more. During these years, Steve worked as Executive Producer and Director of Interactive Services for companies such as Internoded Incorporated and Furniture.com.

Steve is now the President and founder of Hookumu Incorporated, developing highly interactive projects for a broad range of industry leading clientele. He has been working with Flash since it was Future Splash Player (before Macromedia acquired it in 1997), and has developed many award-winning solutions including the Furniture.com Room Planner that was developed while he was at Internoded Incorporated.

Dedication

My Mentors

To Doug and Brian, for helping launch Hookumu and reminding me of the importance of finishing this project. Thank you.

Never-Ending Support

To my wife, Stacie. There isn't enough room in this book or enough words in any language.

Acknowledgments

A great deal of effort by many people went into the writing of this book. The fact is I am just the person in charge of putting the words to paper. In addition to everyone listed in the front of the book, listed below are a number of people who were critical to this book being created. These people include the clients, project leaders, designers, salespeople, accounting people, and everyone involved in each of the companies for each project.

To the Publishers

To Jeff Schultz, Kate Small, Elizabeth Finney, and the rest of the team behind the scenes, thank you, thank you, thank you. Without their abilities to make my words comprehensible and endless ability to keep me motivated, writing this book would never have happened. I only hope that this book is a success for them.

ActionScripting Consultant

Phil Stephenson

Phil was critical to making this book a reality and the biggest thanks possible goes out to him. Not only was Phil involved in the original scripting of many of these projects, but he was also heavily involved in writing of the script descriptions in each chapter. We are extremely lucky to have Phil available as a resource to Hookumu and I also consider Phil a close friend.

Cover Design

Evan Karatzas

Evan is an amazing designer and an even better Creative Director. Many thanks go to Evan for his hard work to produce the cover design. Not only is Evan a friend, but he has recently become a member of the Hookumu team and we look forward to the exceptionally high level of artwork he is capable of producing. Feel free to contact Evan directly if you want to retain his services: evan@ekaratzas.com.

For a Great Idea

Misha Katz

For conceptualizing the original Room Planner idea and making it happen, thank you.

The Clients

A special thanks to each of the clients and companies that allowed us to pull back the curtains and show the workings behind each of their solutions. It is clients such as these that allow us, as a community, to further enable our skills and practices.

An additional thank you goes out to Internoded Incorporated, who is the copyright owner to the Room Planner and who gave us permission to tell the story and distribute the source code so that we can all learn from it. Any questions regarding the Room Planner's use should be directed to Internoded, whose contact information can be found at http://www.internoded.com.

Reaching Me

If anyone has any questions, comments, or thoughts about the book or any of the chapters and their content, please feel free to contact me directly. I would love to hear from you: steve@hookumu.com.

Tell Us What You Think!

As the reader of this book, *you* are our most important critic and commentator. We value your opinion and want to know what we're doing right, what we could do better, what areas you'd like to see us publish in, and any other words of wisdom you're willing to pass our way.

As an Executive Editor for Sams, I welcome your comments. You can email, or write me directly to let me know what you did or didn't like about this book—as well as what we can do to make our books stronger.

Please note that I cannot help you with technical problems related to the topic of this book, and that due to the high volume of mail I receive, I might not be able to reply to every message.

When you write, please be sure to include this book's title and author as well as your name and phone or fax number. I will carefully review your comments and share them with the author and editors who worked on the book.

Email: m3feedback@samspublishing.com

Mail: Jeff Schultz
         Executive Editor
         Sams Publishing
         201 West 103rd Street
         Indianapolis, IN 46290 USA

INTRODUCTION

Designers, Experimenters, and DaVinci's a.k.a. The Introduction

I hope Flash aficionados of every level can take something away from this book. This book was not written for a specific ability level, nor is the goal of this book to take a beginner at Chapter 1 and have them graduate as an expert by the last chapter. For instance, those newer to Flash will likely enjoy some of the basic concepts I cover in the first two chapters. However, those of you who have been working with Flash for some time might find more value in the later chapters.

I do assume that you, the reader, understand the basics of Flash. And I hope everyone, whether a beginner or an expert, can take something away from every chapter. This book is not a tutorial, and I don't cover the fundamental steps in using Macromedia Flash. After all, there are some excellent books available that cover this topic. Instead, I want to show some of the various clients' needs I have encountered and the process involved in deciding on and developing a Flash-based solution for them.

There are a number of developers and designers out there who could easily do as good, if not a better job on the projects I am showcasing here. What I hope is unique about this book is the journey I am taking you through on each project. The journey covers my experiences as a designer, developer, company owner, and project leader, and tells the stories that cover my perspective from each role. I hope that you can use this information to excel on your own, whether on a Flash project, or at a Flash development and design company.

I do dip into some step-by-step procedures, but the main focus is on the overall problem, the solution, and the story behind both. I expect many of you know Flash and ActionScripting better than I do, and I assume that many of you are exceptional designers and animators as well. I hope to cover both the art and technology of the six solutions presented in this book. But, more importantly, I hope that after reading this book, you will better understand how to first define the clients' problem, and then determine the ways in which Flash can be a part of the solution. In addition, I want to reveal the behind-the-scenes thinking, challenges encountered, and discoveries implemented to develop the solution. Each chapter is a story wrapped around an actual client project I have either developed or been involved in developing throughout my career using Flash.

The book should be easy to read and somewhat entertaining. There are no complex devices in place to get through each chapter. However, there is a particular structure used in each case study. The beginning of each chapter has an icon representing the story as being for beginning, intermediate, advanced or professional users. I introduce the players involved in each project, what the client's need was that got us involved in the first place, and we then explore the final solution and the process behind it.

Finally, I close each chapter with a post-mortem in which I discuss how the solution could have been developed better or our approach could have been improved—particularly now that newer technologies are available.

I hope you enjoy the book!

CHAPTER

Intellisync Product Demo

Keep it simple, don't be stupid.

Overview

Flash is a powerful tool that can be used for simple solutions. In this chapter, we will discuss how Flash was used to create a simple product presentation with audio, animations, and basic navigational controls. In addition, we will discuss in brief a couple of additional programs we used to complement Flash. All the challenges we encountered in this project were approached with the understanding that the project had a minimal budget and a compressed timeframe. From the beginning, we knew there would be little time for complex ActionScripting, animations, or custom audio tracks. If you currently have a project to tackle and you have limited resources, I hope this chapter will shed some light on how to utilize Flash and other resources efficiently and effectively to deliver a professional solution. This chapter covers some basic Flash techniques that many of you might already know. What I intend to be the most valuable lesson in this chapter is a peek into how we approached the project and the process we followed to arrive at the final solution.

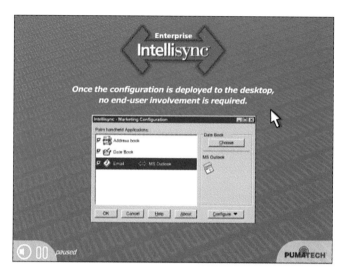

Figure 1.1 *A scene from the final product, showing re-created screen shots and navigational controls.*

The Players

You buy this really cool PDA (Personnel Digital Assistant) for a few hundred dollars so that you can take control of your life. It has a calendar, a date book, a task list, and a couple of games that Atari wouldn't have made twenty years ago. It also has a cradle that you plug into your computer so that you can swap documents and information between your computer and your new Palm, Visor, or Windows CE device. (You'll forgive me if I don't list every manufacturer; the publishers didn't want this book to exceed 400 pages.)

Now if you have ever owned one of these great little devices, you'll know what I'm about to write. You install this software on both your Mac and your PC (after buying another cradle), and you press the synch button for the very first time. You don't get any errors, so everything seems to run smoothly, yea! You excitedly grab the PDA and start exploring, expecting to see every bit of information that's on your computer downloaded to your PDA...wrong.

The software that comes with the PDA synchronizes data between your new device and a program the manufacturers supply to be installed on your PC. The software can't synch your PDA with any other programs such as Outlook, Eudora, and so on. This means your neat little address book and calendar on your new PDA has no information in it. If you want all your contacts and appointments on your new PDA, you have to type them into the new software manually! Because most of us did exist before PDAs and we have many contacts and appointments and because most of us are not willing to spend the next nine or ten days re-entering these contacts into another program, companies started developing synchronization software to address this need. Synching software enables your PDA to talk)to the other programs on your computer and exchange data.

Pumatech is the developer of the leading synchronization software, Intellisync. Okay, now that you have a little background on synchronization software and what it does, let's talk about the project (after all, that's why you bought this book).

At the time that Pumatech contacted us, Hookumu was just a few months old and we were wrapping up our second project. Because we had done a very good job on the project, that client referred Pumatech to us to help with a problem it was having. Intellisync had been an extremely successful software product for the end user and Pumatech was in the process of developing a version for the Enterprise.

Now let me sidetrack for a moment. Most of you are probably far smarter than I, and understand the term *Enterprise*. I heard the term for years before I knew its true definition. In the software world, Enterprise is a category of businesses that are large enough to have internal departments dedicated to nothing more than supporting the company. For instance, when I worked at Furniture.com, we had one group that was responsible for maintaining our email systems and another group that was responsible for installing new software on our computers. It's common for large organizations not to allow the end users—you and me—to install our own software. Instead, they have the internal support teams (typically called Operations) purchase and install the software for you.

PDAs are largely considered a personal item and are typically purchased and installed by the owners, not the companies. See the problem yet? Suddenly these large companies, which have invested large sums of money in teams dedicated to installing and standardizing the software on each machine and to protecting the documents and data that each employee has access to, are under attack by the many different versions of synchronization software being installed on the company computers. Imagine a 200-person company (and this is a small one) in which most of the employees have a PDA. Some have Palms, others have Visors, IPAQs, or Blackberrys, and each has its own version of synchronization software. It is virtually impossible for the Enterprise, the big company, to support all the problems each PDA encounters, let alone all the sensitive corporate data that is now being copied to these tiny little PDAs that can easily be lost at airports, tradeshows, sales meetings, or the kids' soccer game. Being the leading synchronization company that it is, the folks at Pumatech developed a version of the Intellisync software that could easily be installed, configured, and managed by Enterprise-internal IT departments, thereby protecting the corporate data.

The Client's Need: Introducing Enterprise Intellisync

So, I find myself sitting in one of Pumatech's main offices north of Boston, learning of this great new product and all that it can do. I have seen the Web site and, opinion aside, it is of professional caliber and relatively new. I also learned in my research that Pumatech has a relationship in place with the well-known Agency.com group. So, what could I offer that their current providers could not?

Figure 1.2   *The Pumatech identity.*

The problem at hand was that the new software, Enterprise Intellisync, was really just a working prototype; it wasn't even in beta. This is just a part of the process, as the product was not being advertised or sold yet. All the features were not yet functional and much of the product was untested. Pumatech had tackled the hard parts and knew it worked, but now it faced the challenge of communicating the power of this unfinished piece to potential constituents including Pumatech Executives, a select group of clients, and the press.

Because of the fact that I had developed similar solutions for high-tech firms in the past and was familiar with the first-to-market pressures, Pumatech wanted to work with Hookumu to develop a solution that would enable it to demonstrate the product's capabilities before it was ready to stand on its own. To this end, Pumatech was currently sending its Senior Product Manager and a Software Engineer around the country to demonstrate its capabilities armed with a projector and a version of the prototype software on a laptop.

With all the credit going to the exceptional people at Pumatech, and the quality of the products the company develops, the presentation was very well received and starting to generate buzz and interest. The issue Pumatech now faced was how to spread the word faster and how to get these two key traveling presenters back into their offices doing what they do best: further enhancing, producing, and bringing the new product to market.

Hookumu's first task was to better understand the audience—who they are and what information is important to them. Before we could determine the delivery method, we had to understand the audience and their needs. At Hookumu, we accomplish this by drafting a Discovery document that contains an outline of all pertinent information about the project. We didn't want to develop a Web site with a guided tour if the demo was to be given by a channel sales rep who might not always have a dedicated Internet connection. PowerPoint presentations can be very effective, but not if the demo was to be emailed or downloaded from a Web site and self-guided; besides, not everyone has PowerPoint. After a couple of meetings with the Pumatech team, we knew that the demo had to serve two key audiences: those who would receive the demo remotely and guide it themselves, and those who would present the demo to others.

We also knew that in both cases, the audience would already be interested, because they were aware of Pumatech and Intellisync. It was understood that the audience trusted Pumatech and no effort was needed to attract their attention and to define who Pumatech was and what purpose their technology served. This was a nice break from the typical interactive project in which the goal is to explain the technology as quickly and interestingly as possible to viewers who might stray off like kindergarten students in the middle of the demo. Because the Enterprise Intellisync audience knew Pumatech and wanted to understand the new product, they didn't want unnecessary marketing noise.

By this point, we knew Flash was the technology of choice. The demo had to be available as a download, viewable online in a Web page, and had to be small enough to be distributed via email or on a disk. All this was possible via other methods, but considering the short three-week timeframe and the limited budget, we did not have the luxury of creating two or three versions. Because of Flash's ability to author once and distribute via the Web as well as an executable application, it was perfect for this project.

The Solution

Capturing the Demo and Gathering Source Files

I had Kevin Moreno, the engineer who had been giving the demos, install the exact software he used for the demo on my laptop during one of the discovery meetings. I then asked him and Donna Scontsas, the project manager, to present to me the same demo they were giving on the road. In addition to taking notes and stopping the presentation to ask key questions, I took screen shots of every element that I thought had even a remote possibility of making it into the final piece. This would avoid unnecessary trips to the client later in the project.

I had Photoshop open and every time I took a screen shot, I created a new layer and pasted the new screen shot in the document. It ended up being a rather large file, but it provided us with stills of every scene of the demo. I named each layer something unique and, in a Word document, I created a list of each layer name and a brief description of the actions that took place during the scene. For the screen shots, I set the monitor to 800×600 with millions of colors. I wanted as much color depth as possible and I wanted to make sure that I captured as much of the screen action as possible without needing a microscope to see all the elements. Since then, we have discovered a program named Snag-it by TechSmith Corporation. Snag-it is an excellent shareware utility that offers a great deal of control over what onscreen elements you would like to capture, and how you would like to store and organize them. You can find Snag-It at download.com or directly from the developers at techsmith.com.

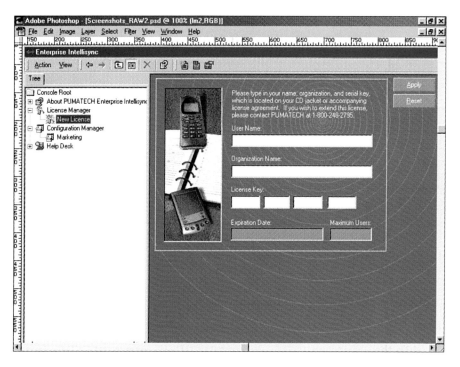

Figure 1.3 *A view of the actual Enterprise Intellisync screen shot taken and stored in Photoshop.*

Now we were armed with all the necessary information to go to work on our own. We had experienced the demo first hand, taken screen shots and notes, and understood the targeted audience and how it would want to use the demo. Had the timeframe and budget both been larger, we would have presented demonstrations to selected users, asked them what information they were looking for, and in general verified the information being presented. However, we were also very confident that the client knew the space and had the message worked out nicely.

Creating a Storyboard

The next step was for us to create a storyboard. Some storyboards can be of Hollywood quality with detailed, realistic sketches and carefully written copy. I never work this way because I find that so much changes between the initial storyboard and the final demo that a great deal of effort can be wasted trying to perfect the initial version.

Instead, I like to capture all the key elements, including the rough message, the order it will be given in, the main navigational elements, and the key animations. Experience, sometimes painful, has taught me that even if we have agreed with the client on the content and how it will be displayed, after the storyboard is in their hands, many revisions will be made. I like to get a working copy into the client's hands quickly so that they can begin to circulate it internally and work out the main issues as soon as possible.

In this case, the client made many excellent suggestions and several rounds of revisions were needed before the storyboard was finalized. This is common and something we planned for from the beginning. After we felt the navigation was set, we asked for a full set of guidelines for the Pumatech brand and moved into look and feel development while the storyboard was still evolving.

Asking the client for any branding guidelines that exist early in the project is an important step. Many companies have gone to great lengths to protect the presentation of their identity and logo. As professional designers, we owe it to the client to follow any guidelines that do exist. I find that typically it is larger corporations that have guidelines and smaller businesses do not. You should see what Lotus Development Corporation has—a three-ring binder with 100 pages of instructions including an attached CD with original files! Even if guidelines do not exist, conduct a little research to find the right person within the company and learn as much as possible about how to work with their brand. This can save you a great deal of time and frustration later in the project. It will also help you establish a positive relationship with the client and can lead to additional work. We have actually won the work to create branding guidelines for companies that do not have them! Of course, we try to develop online interactive versions of such guidelines, but that is another story.

The current storyboard showed that the demo would be about 20 screens long with the first 10 being mostly textual content, the next eight being animated screen shots, and 2–3 more text-based screens. The mix was uncommon, as we usually prefer to have a standard text or visual format throughout a demo. However, we understood the audience and the message and agreed with the current plan.

Keeping a Consistent Design

We decided that if the content was going to change, we wanted to keep the style of the demo consistent. This meant a never-changing background image that would be capable of displaying text messages as well as animated visuals and screen shots.

We now had to decide between a vector or bitmap background image. For file size reasons, I like to use vector designs as much as possible. Although it can be difficult to create vector images that are as deep and attractive as raster images, both Phil Stephenson and I have rather extensive experience in vector illustrations and often create vector backgrounds. Back in the late 1980s, Phil and I worked together at a company producing Yellow Pages ads. As boring and design restrictive as it was, we could use only FreeHand and we had to produce as many as 20 ads per day. It was a phenomenal experience that forced us to become extremely efficient in vector-based design and FreeHand. It is safe to say that Phil is one of the fastest and most proficient FreeHand users today.

Now, Flash is exceptional at creating extremely small files, but what many people do not realize is that vectors, being a series of points, lines, and fills, is a tax on the end user's computer. When you move a vector symbol across the screen in Flash, the viewer's computer has to do an exceptional amount of math to process the movement of each of these points across the screen. In this case, we knew that we would already be re-creating and animating up to eight screen shots in the vector format. Because of this, we did not want to tax the processor by having the screen shots move across a vector created background.

We actually conducted some tests and found that with a few color effects, our relatively fast Pentium III 500MHz machines would start to crawl. Because the background was going to be downloaded only once and then left alone, it was worth the weight of using one giant bitmap for the background at the cost of drastically improved performance. Our challenge was then to create a brand-compliant background that would compress nicely as a JPEG (because every image coming out of Flash is a JPEG), yet was still interesting.

At Hookumu, we design in reverse. We start with designs that have all the bells and whistles with no rules to stifle creativity. We then start analyzing potential designs. Every element in a design should have a reason for existing; if not, it is considered a distraction and removed. Nothing seems more forced in a design than shapes and elements that exist for no reason. We also like to use color as a supportive element, not a major design element. I learned this from the old days of designing logos that needed to look good as a fax copy. If it wasn't a good design in straight black-and-white, it was unlikely that the addition of a fade or color swash would make it much better.

Below are two versions of the design. Although Figure 1.4 was a strong design, we considered it offbrand and we decided showing actual PDAs was a distraction from the core concept of the demo. In a later design, shown in Figure 1.5, we wanted to show the full screen in the monitor but call out to the area of interest. Although successful, we felt that this approach downplayed the completeness of the product and made it feel more like marketing hype.

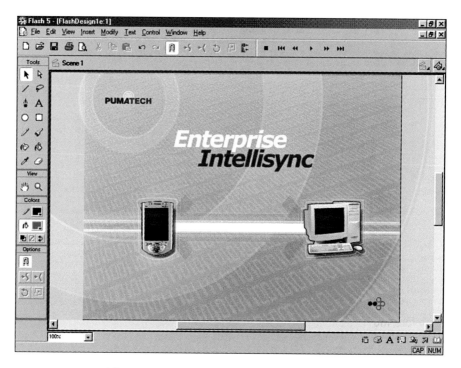

Figure 1.4   *An initial design for the demo.*

For the Pumatech background, the design had to be interesting when nothing but text was over it, yet still be subtle enough for the text to remain legible. We also wanted to add some depth and stay true to our design philosophies. What we ended up with was this color fade from dark blue to Pumatech blue, with a subtle layer of transparent data diffusing into a perspective. The client loved it because it reinforced their brand as reflected in their corporate Web site and added a layer of depth to the demo interface.

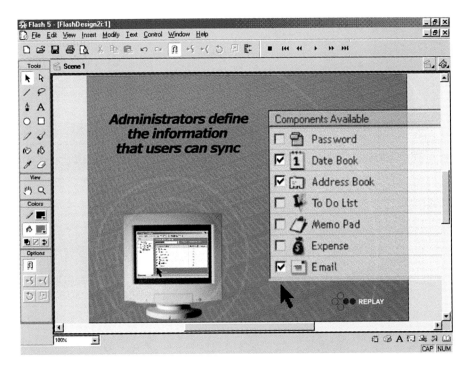

Figure 1.5   *Another early design, this one including the final background.*

Before moving on, we conducted export tests to determine what the best quality setting would be to maintain the correct balance between size and quality. The magic number was 80, which compressed the bitmap from 1MB to 29KB, with little to no noticeable quality degradation. Flash is excellent at compressing well-designed bitmap images. The CD supplied with this book contains the actual Flash authoring file for the Pumatech Enterprise Intellisync demo. It might be a good practice to export the background at various settings to see the impact doing so has on image quality and file size.

Enough preparation. Let's dive into Flash.

15

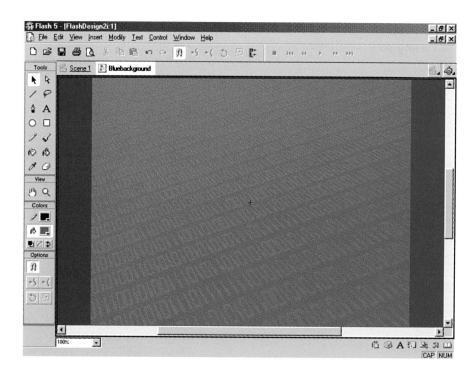

Figure 1.6 *The final background, created in FreeHand and Photoshop.*

Pre-loading Animation

I would like to mention that the pre-loader and opening animations are, almost without exception, the last efforts of the project, testing aside. Our reasoning for this is that these are often the fun and fluff components of every project. A number of unexpected issues can and usually do arise during the meat of the project, and we like to dive in and tackle the core issues prior to dealing with the easier elements. In addition, the core information is really the purpose for the project and developing this first sets the tone and style that we can then reinforce in the pre-loader and logo animation. Without having developed any of the core elements, it is difficult to create a strong pre-loader for the project at hand. For the purpose of this chapter, I think it is appropriate to follow the project from opening scene to closing scene as long as you keep our process in mind.

A pre-loader is an excellent device to use on all your Flash projects. A pre-loader can be a simple `ifframesloaded` script that loads all your elements into memory before playing, or a complex series of scripts that loads and unloads components of your piece as they are needed. In either case, the concept is the same. A pre-loader tells Flash to load all, or a specified amount, of the piece into memory before allowing in the user. This prevents the symbols and artwork and elements in the file from appearing one by one on the stage as they load into memory. There are many readily available examples of how to build good pre-loaders, and we will cover at least two in this book. The pre-loader for this project is a very simple and effective one that includes an elegant animation as well as a status bar.

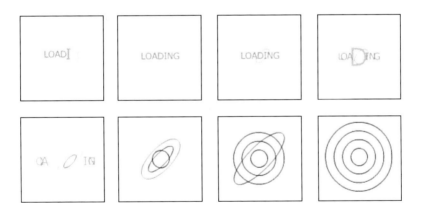

Figure 1.7   *This animation followed the theme of the concentric circles and provided a smooth interesting animation.*

I always recommend giving the user a nice image, animation, or even a bit of information to review as the piece is loading. This keeps the user's attention. However, please spend the time to develop the correct information during the load sequence. If you are trying to load 500KB of information, you know that this might take some time to load and the viewer might be waiting a few minutes, so don't just flash loading on and off the screen. Not only is this incredibly annoying, like the old HTML <blink> tag, but it doesn't tell the viewer anything about how long he must wait, or if in fact the piece is loading at all. On Hookumu.com, we do load external portfolio pieces that are approximately 10KB, and we use a simple "loading" statement for each. Although most viewers will not see it because 10KB loads very fast, the loading statement is in place in case there are some network delays. This is about the only time that a simple loading statement is effective.

If you expect the viewers to wait more than five seconds while the piece loads, spend the time developing information to keep them engaged while they wait. A smooth, interesting animation is essential because it tells the user that the piece is in fact working, and that something is going on behind the scenes. For the Enterprise Intellisync demo, we needed to develop a nice pre-loader that was fast, efficient, and worked well with the overall design of the demo as well as with the Pumatech brand. As you can see in Figure 1.7, we played off of the concentric circles in the logo, had them animate in and out and alternate with the loading text. This pre-loader is small, compliant with the Pumatech brand, and a bit more information than just loading.

In addition to the neat visuals, we included a status bar that tells the viewer how much of the piece has loaded and how much remains. Sometimes we do this with the typical status bar like the one that your browser shows you, and at other times, we do it with a percentage indicator. Later in the book, we will show you how to build a percentage indicator, but for now let's talk about the status bar.

This piece needed to be compliant with both the Flash 4 and Flash 5 plug-ins, so we chose to go with a primarily frame-based pre-loader instead of an ActionScripting-based pre-loader. This allowed us not to worry about which scripting commands were compliant with which version of Flash.

We first established a new scene just for the pre-loader and created a timeline that was 100 frames long. Spanning the length of these 100 frames, we created a simple progress bar that consisted of nothing more than a shape tween. As the piece played from frame 1 to 100, the status bar progressed from left to right.

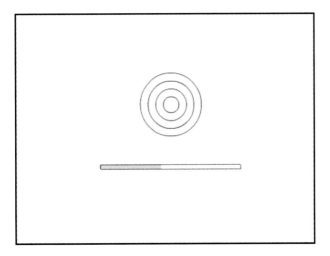

Figure 1.8   *A simple shape tween becomes the status bar.*

We wanted the piece to load and progress in 10% increments, so every 10 frames on a layer called actions, we placed a key frame.

We could have done this in just 20 frames with every two being a 10% segment, but for timeline management purposes, I like to spread things out a little. It does cause a little horizontal scrolling in the timeframe, but the added benefit is the ability to read frame labels. One of the downsides of the Flash timeline is you cannot read frame labels unless the timeline is long enough to display the text.

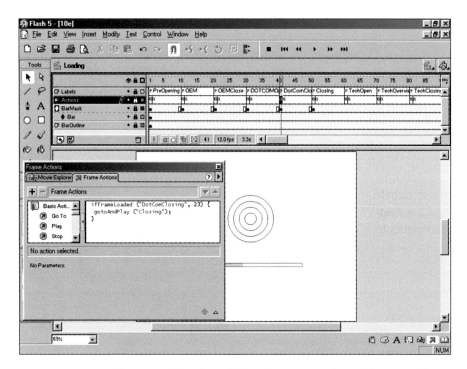

Figure 1.9 *By splitting the progression of the status bar into ten segments, we ensure that the pre-loader will correctly reflect the amount of information loaded regardless of the user's Internet connection.*

We then split all the content in the finished project into 10 relatively evenly sized chunks of content. If the final piece had 10 scenes, this would be very easy because we could load each scene as a 10% increment. It was not true in this case, so we walked through the final piece and identified 10 points in the main timeline that had equal amounts of data. Sometimes it was a scene, other times it was just two or three frames that contained large elements such as the bitmap background. We wrote this information down because we would need it later.

Back in our pre-loader, we added some basic ActionScripting
to load each of the 10 segments we identified. First, we
labeled each of the 10 segments, using names such as
"Audio," "Bitmap," "Opening Animation," and so on. This
helped for organizational purposes. In the first frame of
each pre-load segment, we added the following code:

```
ifFrameLoaded ("SceneName", 30) {
    gotoAndPlay ("Bitmap");
}
```

This simple code says, "Hey, if all the data in a particular
scene ("SceneName") up to a specified frame (30) has been
loaded into memory, go to the next pre-loader frame (in this
case, labeled "Bitmap")." If it has been loaded, Flash goes
to the next pre-loader segment and the progress bar
animates to tell the viewer that data is being loaded. If the
condition is not true and the data has not loaded, Flash
ignores the statements and goes to the next frame, where it
encounters the following script:

```
gotoAndPlay ("CurrentSegment,");
```

`"CurrentSegment"` is the label name of the initial frame of
the current segment. This simply says go back to the frame
we just left, loop between the two until the `ifFrameLoaded`
event is true, and then go to the next of 10 segments
where we do the same thing with new data. This simple,
timeline-based pre-loader is effective, works with Flash 4
and 5, and enables the users to see the status of the
program they are loading.

Another important rule we have is that when a project has
been loaded into memory, we do not abruptly jump the
user to the main screen. Instead, we like to finish the
animation smoothly and then transition the user into the
next scene. Let's talk for a quick moment about how to do
this.

At the beginning of the movie, we use the `set variable`
ActionScript to make the variable `loaded` to equal false like

21

this: `loaded = "false"`. When the end of the pre-loader is reached, we tell the variable loaded to be true: `loaded = "true";`. We then tell the pre-loader timeline to stop, but the loading animation continues to play because it is a movie clip.

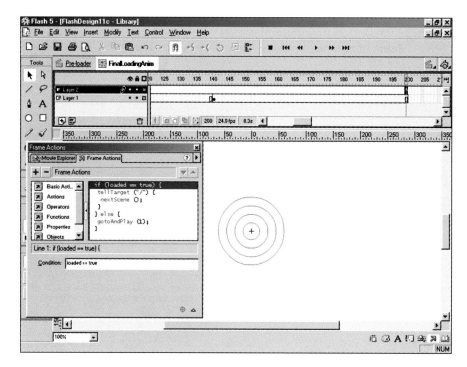

Figure 1.10 *Simple ActionScripting can ensure that your pre-loader animation loops seamlessly.*

In the loading movie clip, we have a frame script at the end of the animation that states

```
if (loaded==true) {
    tellTarget ("/") {
        nextScene ();
    }
} else {
    gotoAndPlay (1);
}
```

This simple script says that if `loaded` equals true (meaning all data has been loaded), tell `"/"` or the main movie line to proceed to the next scene, which is the logo animation scene. If it is not true and all the data has not been loaded into memory, go to frame 1 of this movie clip and keep playing the animation. Simple, easy, and it works!

> *Relative targeting versus absolute targeting: When you use ActionScripting to target, or identify and control, movie clips or other objects, Flash enables you to reference the target using the relative or absolute mode. An easy way to remember which is which is to think of relative as relative to where I am such as, "in my office next to the water cooler." An absolute reference would be "Massachusetts, Boston, 32 Federal Street, 4th Floor, Office 216." Relative targeting comes in handy when you are creating dynamic movie clips with ActionScripting and it is not easy to identify specifically where the movie clip resides.*

Logo Animation

When designing in Flash, we try not to force elements abruptly onto the users' screens and wanted to do the same with the logo and all other elements in this demo. In addition, we try to add to the topic or design at hand so that there is meaning to the animation and not just something that looks cool. Depending on the client, this can be an easy task or one of the largest challenges of the project. Logos are the face of the client and depending on the branding guidelines of a company, clients might allow you to do what is appropriate with the logo for the project, as Pumatech did, or hand you a book the size of the Bible with guidelines on how to use and not use the company logo. If you have ever worked with a large corporation such as IBM or Lotus Development Corporation, you can sympathize with me.

Fortunately, on this project, Pumatech had seen our past work and trusted us enough to, at first, let us do what we thought was best for the project. In this case, it meant adding a small animation that allowed the Pumatech logo to materialize.

Figure 1.11 *The Pumatech logo we needed to work with.*

As you can see, the Pumatech logo is some basic typography with a series of thin, equally weighted concentric circles in the background. One of our immediate concerns was the fact that the concentric circles are not centered in the type, so this could cause some design issues down the road. We made a note and moved on, knowing that now was not the time to sell the client on an upgrade to their identity.

Because this demo was truly about sharing data between multiple sources, we began exploring the use of the concentric circles as radar waves that would carry information from one data source to another. The nature of the circles—small and focused—would allow us to avoid large screen animations that could cause processing and performance issues. In some of the storyboard sketches, we began playing with how these concentric radar circles could be used to attract the user's eye or highlight particular areas of interest. For example, when we wanted the user to follow an onscreen cursor, we had a large concentric circle appear and then scale down to focus on the cursor before we set it in motion. The theme seemed to work and was well received by the client. It was now time to apply it to the appearance of the logo and see how it fit.

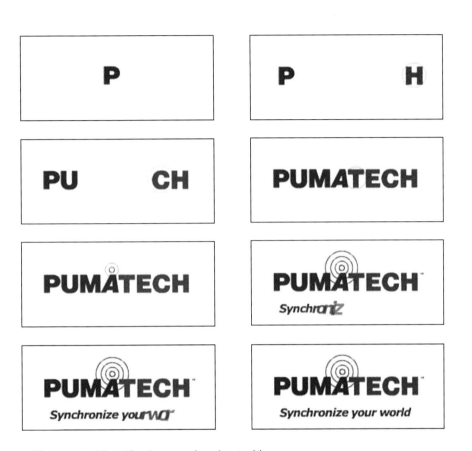

Figure 1.12   *The Pumatech animated logo.*

First, the background colors needed to be determined. I always like to start with neutral to boring colors in the pre-loader, and then I utilize the best background color to emphasize the logo (typically black or white), and then I transition into a nice consistent, attractive background for the demo or Web site at hand. Because the Pumatech logo used a combination of blue and a rust color with thin lines in the logo, we had no choice but white. Decision made. However, using white in combination with the offset radar circles would cause us a problem later when transitioning to the demo background; we will describe this challenge in a moment.

I like logo animations to be brief and simple. We're not trying to win any animation awards here; we want to quickly build the logo onscreen and move on to the core message. Knowing that the consistent theme of radar circles would support the core message, we wanted to utilize them here. Because the type used in the logo is rather common and didn't allow much room for creativity, we decided to stay true to our basic rules and animate each letter with a "popping" concentric radar circle. We worked from the outside in, quickly alternating letters until the logotype was onscreen, and then very quickly animated the centerlines to appear in the same manner. The results were very simple, very quick, and in the client's opinion, very on brand and successful.

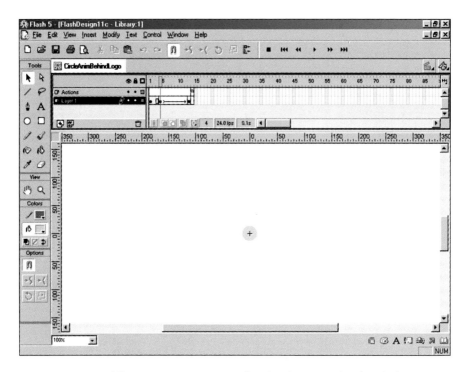

Figure 1.13 *We used a simple tween for the circle animations behind each of the letters in the logo animation.*

To conserve the overall file size, we created one movie clip that is a simple shape tween of a gray circle morphing into a circle line that fades away. This simple animation was used behind each letter of the logo. In the main timeline, we just fired off each movie clip, one after another. To accomplish this, we simply established a new keyframe each time we needed another letter to animate, and placed a new instance of the gray circle animation behind a letter in the logo. We placed a stop action in the last frame of the gray circle MC to ensure the gray circle MC did not continue looping. Building the MC this way would never allow us to have the Gray Circle MC continuously loop, but we knew that we would never need this functionality. Another option would be to have no stop actions and tell the MC in the main timeline to behave like a graphic and play just once.

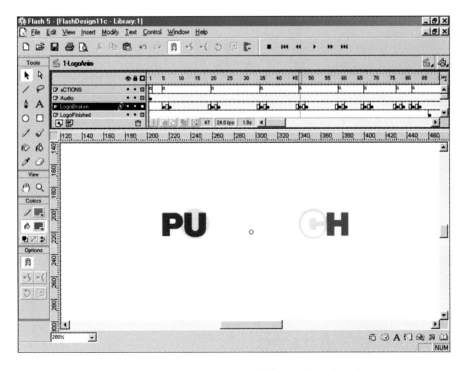

Figure 1.14 *Note the repetitive use of the circle animation in the main timeline.*

What we learned is that for some reason, movie clips are the most efficient symbol to use. Buttons and graphics tend to weigh more even if the contents are identical. So, we try to use movie clips as much as possible. Because of this, we had to ensure that the movie clip did not loop. Knowing that we would most likely not reuse this clip, we placed a stop action in the last frame. This way we did not have to use instance names and ActionScripting to control the timelines in the various movie clips. Instead, we just tell it to stop and forget about it.

Swishhhhhhhh

Most of you by now are aware of the great little text animation program called Swish, by David Michie and Hung-Hsin Chang. This mini-Flash-like program automates the tedious step-by-step frame animation process. If you want text to slide in from the left one letter at a time, wait three seconds, and then explode, Swish can do that for you in just a couple of clicks. Swish is available from www.swishzone.com, and I highly recommend that all designers cough up the $30 for this tool. The time savings is well worth the money.

At the time we were building this demo, Swish had not been out very long and we were having a blast creating quick little text effects in no time. We couldn't resist the urge to use it. Now, don't get me wrong. Swish is a great tool to have in your arsenal, but it is a very popular program, and its limited number of easy effects are starting to appear everywhere.

This ubiquity is one downside of Swish; the other is the file size produced. Swish outputs a SWF that you then import into your main movie. The problem is that the file is a series of frames with individual elements. Very few of the effects use symbols, and therefore, a couple of simple text animations could quickly inflate your overall file size. There are some great designers out there utilizing the more advanced features of Swish to create unique animations. If you take the time to experiment, Swish can offer more than what most of us use it for.

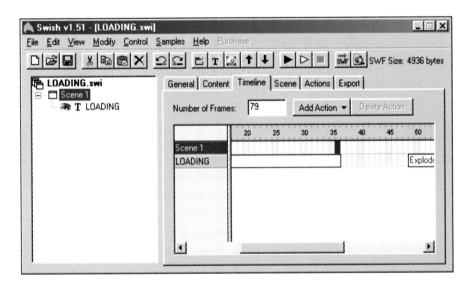

Figure 1.15 *Swisssssh. Quick and easy-to-use interface.*

The benefit is great on projects with short timeframes and small budgets. I think our first design presentation to the client of the EI Demo had something like twelve Swish effects in it. We knew we would not keep them all, but it was so fun, easy, and quick to use, we couldn't resist.

Figure 1.16 *Swish enables you to see the effects in progress as you build them.*

The final demo uses three or four of the Swish effects and we tried to be conservative and consistent throughout the demo. Without Swish, we would not have had the time to hand tween so many text animations.

Adding the Audio Pops

Where we did get a little more complex is in adding audio for each "popping" letter. One of Flash's strengths is that there are many ways to handle audio. Later in this chapter, we will discuss our overall plan for audio in this project, but for the logo animation, we wanted one audio file to play each time a logo letter appeared.

At first, we simply put one instance of the audio clip titled "drip" into the main timeline when any letter appeared. But later on, when we determined that there would be many audio effects as well as some ambient audio, we wanted to offer the end user the ability to control the audio. If we had a bunch of rogue effects scattered about the timeline, it would be a tedious and complex process to ensure that every instance could be controlled. If we had added audio the way we initially planned, the "Stop all Sounds" script would stop any current sound, but the next time the timeline encountered a sound, it would play. We wanted to give the user the ability to mute all sounds and later turn them back on.

Our solution was to create one movie clip for all audio effects; we called this movie clip "sounds." It was always on the stage and we always gave it an instance name of "sounds."

Instances can be a very powerful Flash device. Using instances, you can individually name movie clips on the stage and control them through ActionScript. Sources such as the Flash manuals, the book *Sams Teach Yourself Macromedia Flash 5 in 24 Hours* by Phillip Kerman, and online sources such as www.flashkit.com are excellent

resources to learn more about instances and other core
Flash concepts.

Our sound movie clip contains no visible elements, just a
timeline and a series of audio effects. This allowed us to
just dump the movie clip on the stage and not worry about
where it is positioned or what it might be blocking. All we
had to do was ensure that it was present and had an
instance name of "sounds."

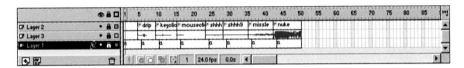

Figure 1.17 *A peak into timeline of the sound movie clip.*

As you can see, we had three layers in this timeline. One
layer for frame labels (one label for each sound), one layer
for the actual sound effect, and one layer for actions. Any
good Flash resource will tell you that it is good planning to
have a layer dedicated to actions.

The way it works is that when we need an effect in the
main movie timeline, we just tell the instance "sounds" to
go to the appropriately labeled sound effect and play.

```
tellTarget ("sounds") {
    gotoAndPlay ("drip");
}
```

In the "sounds" movie clip, one frame after each sound
effect is encountered, an action tells the movie clip to go to
frame 1 (where there is no sound) and stop. This allows the
current sound effect to continue playing and prepares the
"sounds" movie clip for the next effect it needs to play
when called. In this simple timeline, the action for each
sound is simply gotoAndStop (1);.

There are many ways this can be done and I am sure that some of you ActionScripting gurus will find better ways than with this example. But if your project does not call for any complex ActionScripting, particularly sound, this simple solution is quick and efficient. Later in this book, we discuss more advanced ways to control audio. The remainder of the Logo animation is just a simple timeline with the appropriate elements appearing on stage at the appropriate times. Feel free to reference the included source file on the attached CD to see how we did it. I'd now like to move on to the full-screen transition challenge we faced.

Full-Screen Transitions

As we mentioned earlier, we like to start with neutral colors for the pre-loaders, move to an appropriate color for the logo presentation—usually black or white—and then into an interesting, consistent background for the main content. In general, the purpose for this is to build interest so that when the user is in the main content of the demo it is very engaging. It also enables us to start with an efficient pre-loader so that the user only has to wait for the important information. The challenge this adds is that at some point you are forced to use a full-screen transition from the pre-loader to the logo presentation to the main background.

Although full-screen transitions might work great on your Pentium XX 2000MHz machine, most people do not have extremely powerful machines and if you do not want them to experience delays, you need to plan for a transition that the targeted user can enjoy.

The first transition everyone seems to try is the full-screen alpha fade from the solid color to the bitmap background. You will quickly find that this is probably the worst possible transition you could force your users through, particularly if you have multiple bitmap and vector symbols on the screen, and it's even worse if those elements have effects in them. For the Pumatech demo, we experimented with this type of transition on our targeted machines, a 200MHz Pentium and a Power Macintosh 8000/100, and quickly ruled it out because it was too slow.

We started experimenting with various types of transitions: multiple squares fading out like transparent tiles; reveal fades like barn doors sliding open; one very interesting effect in which the white background is actually a series of nickel-shaped dots that shrink away from the upper-left corner to the lower right. This last effect was quite interesting and required a bit of intelligent ActionScripting to pull off, and it was even very fast. The problem was that it was more like a "bubble" effect and the client did not prefer it.

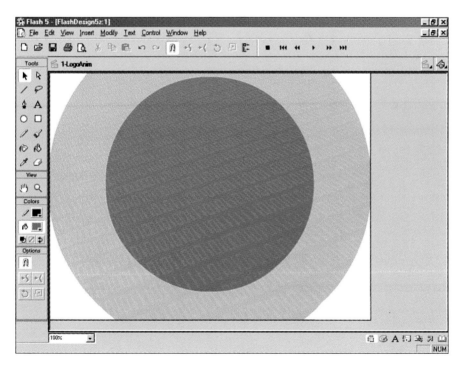

Figure 1.18   *The WB effect that was left on the cutting room floor.*

What we learned in all our experiments is that good transitions, ones that performed well on all machines and were basically invisible to the viewer, are those that moved a plain shape off the screen. Now we don't mean a grouped square or a symbol, but a completely broken-apart simple shape such as a square or circle. Staying true to the radar circle theme, we developed a transition that utilized a single white circle that was larger than the stage. When we wanted to reveal the background, we used a simple shape tween from 100% to a size so small that it wasn't noticeable.

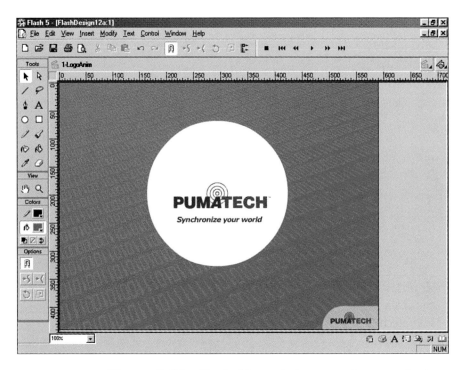

Figure 1.19 *The last frame before we swipe away the logo with the white transition.*

This shape tween was the most efficient approach and didn't cause any performance issues. We did, however, have some alignment problems, because as we mentioned earlier, the concentric circles in the Pumatech logo are not centered. This was detectable when the circle from the transition was equal in size to the circles in the logo. We resolved the problem by having the logo disappear when the circle reached the outer P and H of the logo. It made for a very nice transition.

Enter Audio

As the main screen transitions in, we want the audio to begin playing. Let's talk about the external audio file for a minute. In most cases, looping background audio files can easily be 30% of the overall file size, if not more. In the case of this demo, the demo SWF file is 400KB and the audio SWF is 60KB. This is a significant amount of the overall piece just for some neat elevator music. Now, I agree that audio can greatly enhance the user's experience but in this case, the audio is a nice touch, but not an essential element.

We certainly do not want the users to have to wait for the audio if they do not want it. In addition, we wanted to give users the ability to turn the audio on and off at any time. Because of this, we choose to load the audio file as an external SWF file.

To avoid any performance issues, we begin loading the audio several frames prior to the screen transition. In the appropriate frame, we simply call out to the same directory the main file is in to load the audio.swf file. This allowed Pumatech to ship the two files together and not have to worry about their locations or directory structures. We also knew that sometimes Pumatech would not want to send the audio file along, as when they knew the viewer would not care for audio or when bandwidth was a concern. We also knew that the user might inadvertently misplace the audio file or place it in another directory. To ensure that the piece was functional and did not appear broken no matter what the scenario, we included the audio controls in the actual audio file. This way if the audio.swf is not present and doesn't load, the user doesn't even know the difference. No audio, no controls!

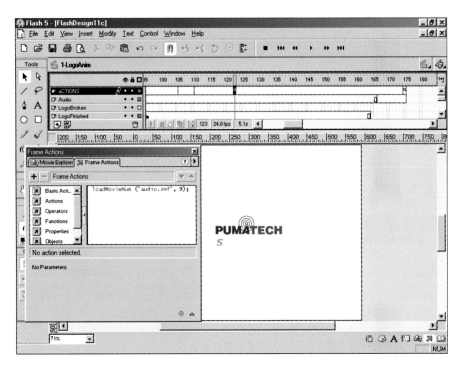

Figure 1.20 *Bring on the tunes.*

For this demo, there was neither sufficient time nor budget to use Re-Birth or GrooveMaker to author our own custom composition. This doesn't mean we had to sacrifice quality. All it meant was we had to be willing to use general audio, with a short loop that could seamlessly play in the background. There are many readily available resources for stock audio, including Eyewire.com and FlashKit.com. In this example, we used loops available on FlashKit.com because the loops are presented in actual SWF files, making it easy to browse and narrow down the selection. We chose a piece that is only a few seconds in length, mellow, and looped rather seamlessly.

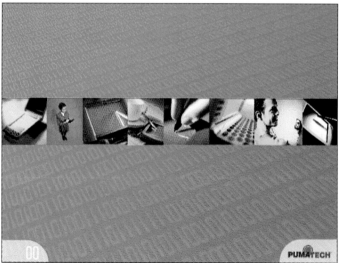

Figure 1.21 *With the audio loaded and without the audio loaded. Notice that there are no audio controls when the audio isn't loaded.*

Editing the Audio

We downloaded the audio in MP3 format because that is the fastest and cleanest format. We still prefer Macromedia SoundEdit 16 for editing raw audio files, so we first had to convert the MP3 to WAW format because SE16 does not support MP3. Although SE16 is still a tool of choice among designers and developers, it is in need of an upgrade. Also, sorry PC users, but SE16 is Mac only. PC users might want to try SoundForge by SonicFoundry. I rely on my Mac for manipulation of the audio so, unfortunately, I can't tell you much about PC sound tools.

To convert the audio, we utilized a simple PC shareware utility called GoldWave, which is available at www.goldwave.com. If you're only on a Mac, there are many utilities available so just sniff around a little. After the file was in WAV format, we brought it back over to our Mac for editing in SE16. In SE16, we played with the overall tempo until it matched the demo's style and cleaned up the entry and exit notes so that the looping would be seamless. We then saved it as a WAV file and brought it back into Flash on the PC. In Flash, we made the audio SWF stage the same size as the main file. This made it easy to position the audio controls in the main movie. We then created a simple speaker button and added the following script:

```
on (release) {
    _Level0:sound = "false";
    gotoAndStop ("AudioOff");
}
```

In the main timeline of the "Audio" file, we simply labeled another frame "AudioOff," added a stop frame action, and removed the audio from that frame. This is a simple audio control mechanism, but it is very effective.

A Bigger, Unplanned Challenge

I would prefer to avoid mentioning one problem we encountered and pretend that we are flawless experts, but this book is about real-world case studies, and in the real world, you will encounter problems. In the real world, you will have to develop workarounds in time- and budget-sensitive situations. Hopefully, you can benefit from hearing about a problem we encountered and learn from the workaround we implemented.

As we mentioned, the ambient audio was loaded as an external source, and the sound effects, such as mouse clicks and swish effects, were loaded in their own internal movie clip titled "sounds." This was done by myself working on one component of the piece and by Phil working on another. It was only at the end, when we were implementing the ambient audio and the mute feature, that we realized the effects were not being muted. This is because the mute feature says "stop all sounds" and "stop all sounds" works only for sounds currently playing. When we tell new sounds such as effects to play, the mute feature no longer truly works as the user would expect it to.

We explored putting the sound effects in the ambient audio movie and calling out to them as needed. This would have caused issues with the timeline jumping to various places at once; for instance, if the user unmuted at a point where both an effect and the ambient audio had to play. We didn't have the time to properly implement and debug this type of solution because the deadline was nearing. The client had already approved each instance of the effect and we did not want to kick off a repetitive round of QA. Phil came up with a simple solution that worked with our current sound effects design.

The main timeline of the movie had a unique layer called "audio." On this layer, we had just one symbol: a movie clip called "sounds" with an instance name of "sounds." As mentioned earlier, when we wanted to play an effect, we simply told the "sounds" movie clip to go to the appropriate effect and play it. All we had to do was find every action in the main timeline that called out to the sound clip to play, and add the following script:

```
if (/:sound eq "true") {
    tellTarget ("sounds") {
        gotoAndPlay ("mouseclick");
    }
}
```

We already implemented the variable that checked whether the audio was true or false, based on whether the user muted the audio. We simply added a check in each call for an effect and said, "Hey, if audio is true, go ahead and play the effect; if not, the user wants it muted and play nothing." For QA, all we had to do was ensure that when the audio was muted, no effects at all were playing!

The Client Adds a Challenge

In the discovery phase, we determined that this would be a looping presentation and no navigational controls were needed. Guess what? At the last stage of the project, at about the same time we were implementing the sound effects patch, the client determined that having the ability to pause the presentation made sense!

Now, pausing a Flash file is a simple matter. However, when movie clips are embedded in movie clips you have a problem because movie clips keep playing when the main timeline is stopped. We tackled the issue of implementing an unplanned pause button into the interface easily enough. The interface was extremely simple, and we knew how to easily pause the main timeline. The challenge was how to pause *every* movie clip—including the audio— simultaneously and indicate to the user that the file was paused. Not to mention that when played again, every element had to remain synchronized and instantly start playing.

First, let's tackle the state of the paused indicator.

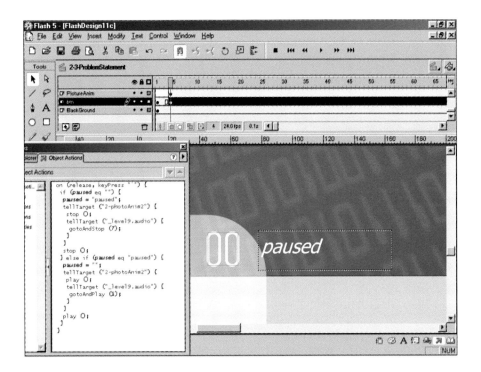

Figure 1.22   *For this project, it doesn't get more complex than this.*

Next to the pause button, we created a small dynamic text field, gave it a variable name of "paused," and embedded the text "paused" into it. The script attached to the pause button gave us the ability for the text "paused" to appear next to the pause button any time we chose:

```
on (release, keyPress "`") {
    if (paused eq "") {
        paused = "paused";
        stop ();
        tellTarget ("_level9.audio") {
            gotoAndStop (7);
        }
    } else if (paused eq "paused") {
```

```
            paused = "";
            play ();
            tellTarget ("_level9.audio") {
                gotoAndPlay (1);
            }
        }
    }
```

Ignore all this script; we will explain the rest in a moment. These two simple pieces of code tell the dynamic text block to display the word paused (paused = "paused";) or display nothing (paused = "";). That's it, it's that simple.

Now let's talk about the button script and controlling the audio. We gave the button a simple on mouse event command and included an on key press command for presenters who wanted simply to press the ` key to pause the presentation. This script says to check the paused variable when the user pushes the pause button. If paused equals nothing, meaning there is no text in the display field, the movie is playing, so do the following: Stop the main timeline and tell the ambient audio file we loaded into level 9 to go to its mute frame number 9. The statement paused = "paused"; simply tells the dynamic text to display the word paused. Everything stops and all is great.

If the movie were paused already (and paused did equal "paused"), when the user pushed the button, it goes to the else if script, tells the dynamic text to display nothing (""), tells the main movie line to play, and tells the main ambient audio to go to frame 1 and play, which will reinitiate the ambient audio. Everything starts replaying, including ambient audio and all is great, except...

The preceding script is from a section of the movie when no other movie clips are present. If they were present, this button would pause only the main timeline and every other movie clip would continue playing. To fix this, we had to roll up our sleeves and do some manual labor.

The solution was to step through the movie and every time
there was a movie clip on the stage, give it an instance
name and add a key frame in the button layer so that we
could have a unique instance of the pause button.

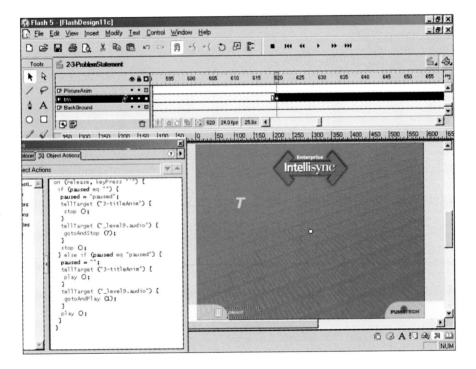

Figure 1.23   *This code enables us to pause the audio and
the motion onscreen.*

For this example, we show the button where the presenting
explosion occurs. Here is the script:

```
on (release, keyPress "`") {
    if (paused eq "") {
        paused = "paused";
        tellTarget ("3-titleAnim") {
            stop ();
        }
```

```
        tellTarget ("_level9.audio") {
            gotoAndStop (7);
        }
        stop ();
    } else if (paused eq "paused") {
        paused = "";
        tellTarget ("3-titleAnim") {
            play ();
        }
        tellTarget ("_level9.audio") {
            gotoAndPlay (1);
        }
        play ();
    }
}
```

This should look familiar. We tell each movie clip instance on the stage to stop. In this case, only the clip titleanim is on stage, so it is easy enough. However, if there were 12 movie clips on stage, we would need to call out each instance and tell it to stop; when unpaused, we would need to call each out and tell it to play.

Now, I know this solution is a bit rudimentary and we will cover more complex solutions later, but this patch not only worked perfectly, it also is a good example of a workaround that didn't require complex coding. I am not an ActionScripting expert and these solutions are helpful to me when I do not have my team available to help. If you're looking to dig into really complicated code, wait until we show you some of the code in the Room Planner!

That's primarily it for this case study. I would like to mention that FreeHand was utilized a great deal for the screen shot re-creations when we could not get Flash to trace or break them apart legibly. I suppose that Adobe Illustrator would work as well, but the SWF export in FreeHand is very convenient. As tedious as it was, we created as many symbols as possible of the many browser and Windows devices. This not only reduced overall file size

but also allowed for speedy development in the future
when other screen shots are needed in Flash and bitmaps
are not desirable.

Final Touches

When the project was approved, we added some final
touches, such as a disk version that used the FSCommand
feature to enable the user to quit, and we developed an
icon for the .exe file.

FSCommand is an easy-to-use piece of ActionScripting that
allows the movie's host environment—such as the Flash
player in this case or the Web browser in other cases—to
communicate with the movie. For the disk-based version of
the EI Demo (not the Web version) we entered an
FSCommand to a quit button on the final screen as follows:

```
on (release) {
    fscommand ("quit");
}
```

This simple command tells the Flash player to quit when
the button is released. Other FSCommands include
fullscreen, which enlarges the player to fill the screen, and
allowscale, which allows the user to resize the window. For
more information about FSCommand, refer to the Flash
ActionScript Reference Guide.

The final demo would primarily be distributed via disk or
email, so we wanted to add a little finesse and create an
icon. To do this, we used version 4.5 of the program
AXIALIS AX Icons. It is a simple 32×32, or 16×16, or 8×8
icon drawing program. You can easily create, copy, and
paste icons, and when they are done, you can save them
into the final Flash .exe file. We chose to use the Intellisync
red arrow as our icon. It was tempting to use the concentric
circles, but that was *our* theme and the demo was for the
product, which has its own logo.

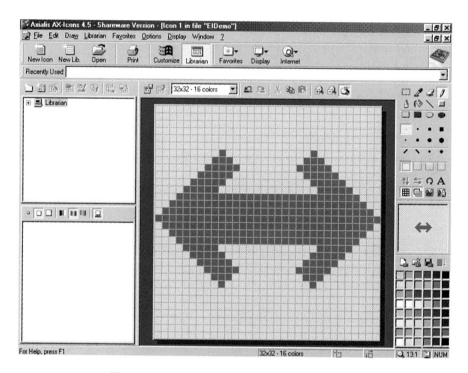

Figure 1.24 *AX Icons makes it easy to put a professional icon on your final files.*

Post-Mortem

Looking back, we learned a great deal from this project. The biggest lesson, which we always try to practice, is that the most essential phase to any project is planning. Had we taken into account the possibility of global muting and pausing, we would have built in simple devices to avoid the laborious ActionScripting we were forced to endure at the end of the project. We now plan for these in advance of every project, regardless of the client's need for pausing, muting, or any other global function. Surprisingly, it is still more efficient to take the time to plan and code it properly in the beginning than to solve the problem by any other means!

Time constraints never did allow us to create custom text animations. Although I am pleased with our limited use of Swish, I do flinch every time I see the presenting animation with the exploding Swish effect. Given the chance, I would probably choose to redesign this section with something a bit more unique. But Swish was fun, and allowed us more than we could have hand-built.

This case study was in development as Flash 5 was in release, so we switched authoring environments in the middle of the project. This can be a risk, but we did extensive testing. In this case study, we talk about one particular piece of ActionScripting that is now outdated: the `Telltarget` command.

`Telltarget` is now deprecated in Flash 5, which means that it is still fully functional, but Macromedia has created a more efficient means of handling such situations and encourages use of a newer function or syntax. In this case, Macromedia suggests and encourages the use of the `with` syntax. Other deprecated and updated functions include `ifFrameLoaded` and `updateAfterEvent`. The actions window has a feature that enables you to highlight those syntaxes that have been deprecated. It is a good idea to become familiar with these newer functions because I am sure that Macromedia will phase out the deprecated ones in future releases.

All in all, the project was very successful, on time, on budget, and facilitated the client in presentations of the product, which was the ultimate goal. We never could have built such a dynamic presentation using PowerPoint, Director, or traditional HTML. I hope one of the things you take away from this chapter is how to determine when it is appropriate to use Flash.

CHAPTER

George the Cat Holiday Card

Simply Viral Marketing.

Overview

Flash can be used to simulate applications without any complex coding. In this chapter, I will discuss how Flash was used to create a simple and fun marketing game for Furniture.com at the holidays. This very simple solution, designed to be delivered as a stand-alone .exe instead of in a Web browser, will show that even the newest Flash designers can build engaging and interactive applications with just a basic understanding of ActionScripting. I will also cover some basic character animation techniques implemented.

Figure 2.1 *George and the snowman chill out.*

The Players

To understand the needs of the client and the project, let's take a look at the events surrounding it. The project for this case study took place at the height of the dot-com craze. Back in the fall of 1999, there was this notion that the Internet was the next great, unexplored frontier and the spoils went to the first pioneers to stake their claim. Dot-com businesses were being launched daily; if you had a business idea, you could start an Internet business. If you had an Internet business with a killer URL, such as Furniture.com, you could attract a great deal of investment money. Venture capitalists were funneling a great deal of money into dot-com companies and the companies were finding ways to spend it, fast. Now don't get me wrong, a large amount of effort by some exceptional people goes into building a business and a plan that can attract millions of dollars from investors. But because this book is not about sound business models and investing, we can have some fun with it!

Pets.com, Cars.com, Realtor.com, Weddings.com, Amazon.com, BN.com, News.com, Software.com, Dot.com: The list is never ending. And within each market, such as pet supplies, there were five or six companies fighting for customers and Web traffic to be the market-leading dot-com company.

As both a consultant serving these clients and later as a member of one of the dot-com companies I must say it was very invigorating. Money and profits were no longer the main concern. What really mattered was being the first to market and attracting the most Web traffic. To do this, companies were spending millions of dollars on marketing. After all, to make the online sale, you had to get the traffic. And to get the traffic, you had to let the world know you existed, and to do that you had to have marketing.

You all know what I am talking about. You've seen or heard about the Super Bowl commercials: $2 million for a 30-second spot. Now imagine being a new company with no profits and spending $2 million on a commercial! As a consumer, it was exciting to have so many companies spending so much venture capital money to attract our attention, get us to go look at their site, and hope that we would eventually buy a 25-pound bag of dry dog food.

In the case of this chapter, I'm not talking about pet supplies, but instead furniture such as couches, leather chairs, dining room sets, and chaise lounges. (Since working at Furniture.com, the chaise lounge has now become my favorite piece of furniture.) We had just launched the first release of the Room Planner, which is a great project I will

51

talk about in the last chapter of the book, so we were of course very familiar with the company. But until this point, I had been dealing strictly with Misha Katz, the founder of Furniture.com. Now it was the marketing department that was calling.

The Client's Need: Introducing George the Cat

Figure 2.2 *The Furniture.com logo.*

So, now I suddenly find myself sitting in the dining room of Furniture.com preparing for a meeting with the marketing department. Dining room, you ask? I should mention that Furniture.com had some of the coolest offices I have ever seen. The floor plan was huge, so they took the center of this giant floor and turned it into a house. Inside the house was a variety of conference rooms, such as a dining room and living room, completely furnished and decorated by interior designers. The cafeteria was the kitchen and we even had an indoor patio complete with patio tables and real wood decking. The main entrance to the building was a residential entryway with a doorknocker and mailbox. The outside of the house (which was still inside on the main floor) was completely covered in vinyl siding with an actual roof, shingles, spot lights, and even a garage (where fabric swatches were kept) and a basketball hoop. Remember we're talking about venture capital money here.

I had been here many times throughout the Room Planner project, but it was always for brief meetings with Misha or the technical teams. I was now sitting in the dining/conference room, which is the same room used for board meetings. It's a beautiful room with a large mahogany dining room table in the middle. Sitting around the table were a variety of marketing people including the vice president and director of marketing. A laptop was hooked up to a projector and a large sketchpad was on an easel in the corner of the room. It was clear they were preparing to cover a lot of information in this meeting.

For the next two hours, I was introduced to Furniture.com's newest marketing campaign, George the Cat.

Figure 2.3   *Debonair with an attitude, George the Cat.*

In the spirit of the Pets.com sock puppet, Furniture.com had a new company spokesperson, or a spokescat. Hopefully you saw these commercials; they were all on primetime TV for several months. They included this lazy cat that could speak and never left the house. He had impeccable taste and designed his home to be so comfortable that he had no reason to leave.

The print, radio, and TV campaigns were in production and now Furniture.com needed an online presence for George. Like Pumatech (refer to Chapter 1, "Intellisync Product Demo"), Furniture.com employed several of the largest Internet consulting firms as vendors including iXl, Sapient, and US Web/CKS (now marchFIRST). Again, I was confused as to why Furniture.com would not use one of these vendors to produce the site.

In this case, it wasn't a matter of budget, but instead of time. George was to be launched in the next week and a half, and he needed to be on the Internet by then. Furniture.com didn't feel the larger firms could have something up and running in that timeframe. Because of the fast and professional work we had done on the Room Planner, they approached us, Internoded Incorporated, with this project. Build a site in less than two weeks to mirror a national marketing campaign? No problem.

But wait—there's more.

We conducted the discovery meeting at that same time, one of my conditions for accepting the project. During this meeting, they talked about how a direct e-mail campaign would be targeted at current Furniture.com registered users to draw traffic to the site. At this point, I saw an opportunity. The goal of www.georgethecat.com was to attract new users who might not have heard of Furniture.com and direct them to the Furniture.com site, thereby increasing traffic and eventually sales. The problem was if the e-mail campaign was directed at registered Furniture.com users, how would the company generate new traffic?

I came up with the idea of sending users a fun puzzle that, when solved, offered a coupon; these users could pass the puzzle on to their friends who might not be aware of Furniture.com. This type of solution is often referred to as a *viral marketing campaign* because of the way the solution spreads like a virus.

Furniture.com loved the idea and now we were charged with the task of developing both a Web site and an interactive e-mail application in less than two weeks.

The Solution

The final solution was a Flash application delivered as a stand-alone .exe file that was e-mailed to everyone on the Furniture.com customer list. We called it the George the Cat Interactive Holiday card, and it was an exceptional success in attracting new customers. Let's talk more about how we developed the solution.

Understanding George and Gathering Source Files

The marketing folks at Furniture.com were really a great team and developed an in-depth profile of George outlining his attitude and personality. This all translated very well into the TV and radio campaigns set to launch with the new Web site and e-mail campaign. It was our job to capture all this information and communicate it online.

I don't want to go into detail about the site, and it is no longer available since Furniture.com ceased operations, but I would like to briefly mention that the site was a success. It included sections all about George, and an area where you could see and hear both the radio and TV ads. One of the most popular sections was the Talk to George feature. You could e-mail George, and occasionally there were even live chats with George. We had an excellent writer at

Furniture.com who posed as George when corresponding with people who wrote in. We had some interesting e-mails from people (mostly kids, but we would often get e-mails from people's pets)! We answered every e-mail and it was fun.

The decision to build and maintain this site was not easily determined. Because George would be viewed as a Furniture.com representative, anything he said, did or didn't do would reflect directly on Furniture.com. To emphasize that point, we needed to ensure that the site would be easy for the client to update and maintain by using simple technologies. We also needed to ensure that as long as the e-mail account for George was active and advertised, someone was properly reviewing and responding to the mail.

Let's get on with the project. We had all these great source files, but they all were movies, pictures, or voice tracks—no caricature of George existed. Money was not a major issue, but time was and we were concerned that if we attempted to draw George, we would spend the whole two weeks tweaking George until Furniture.com thought he was perfect.

To take advantage of the approaching holiday season, we quickly came up with the snowman idea. We wanted to stay away from any particular religious theme but focus instead on snow and the holidays in general. So, the idea was to have a snowman-building contest; if you built a snowman George liked, he would reward you with a coupon. While you built the snowman, George heckled you from the window of his house. Remember George does not leave home; he is not "an outdoor cat." George would never consider going out into the dirty world and associating himself with the outdoor felines. George had too much taste and built his environment to be too comfortable to leave. George would never consider himself an indoor cat either; he simply was human. Or so he thought.

With time ticking away, we started planning the interactivity of the game. We knew we had to build several options for the snowman's hat, eyes, nose, and other pieces, and we still had to build in the interactivity and test the piece. We were starting to feel the pressures of time.

We decided to spend $1,000 of the budget to hire a cartoon artist who sketched three different versions of George. Each version of George had him in a variety of different poses. This is a great example of time savings. Although we could have created interactive George ourselves, we're not caricature artists and it would have taken many revisions to please the client. After the client picked a sketch they liked, it would be very easy for us to create George based on the sketch.

We then presented the sketches to Furniture.com and told them to pick one of the three. As expected, they started discussing the possibility of doing even more drawings and having George in different poses. We told them that this wouldn't be a problem, but that it would extend both the budget and the deadline. As soon as they heard this, they were more than happy with the sketches presented. This is called "client management." It's not that the three original sketches weren't good enough—it's just human nature to want to explore and revise, particularly if you are an artist or in marketing!

The artist was so good, in fact, that we had him sketch the scenery for the piece as well. Keep in mind that he drew just the sketches. We did the actual final artwork in FreeHand, manually tracing and re-creating the scanned-in sketches and then exporting the artwork to Flash. This proved to be fast and affordable and allowed us to focus on development.

Figure 2.4   *George up close.*

Keep It Organized

It's worth noting that the project ended up with more than two hundred symbols and Movie Clips. To keep development time to a minimum, we planned on how we would organize the information from the beginning. This is an important step on any project because it will save time and confusion in the long run when you are searching for the correct symbol when you need it.

Flash allows you to create folders inside of the Library to help organize your symbols. We like to keep all symbols inside a folder for organizational purposes. For this project, we created folders for all the George elements, folders for each of the character themes, another for music files, and, as best practice, we created a folder to store miscellaneous symbols.

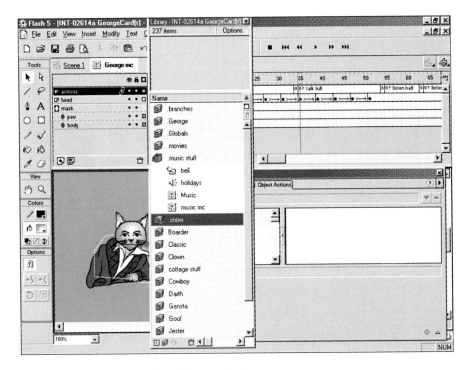

Figure 2.5   *Let's keep it organized.*

In addition to folders, it is helpful to use a standard naming convention. Flash displays folders and symbols in alphabetical order inside the library. For symbols that we need to access often, we start the name of the folder with a period. Flash then always displays these folders at the top of the library, making it quick for us to locate the symbol and maximizing our development time.

Animating George

After the client approved the digital rendition of George, we needed to bring George to life. Remember George never leaves the house, so we designed him leaning out a window wearing a Hugh Hefner–like robe. George's body is just a static Movie Clip with no animation. We did want George's head to be animated. To do so, we decided to have three states of his head: one looking at the user; one looking partially at the snowman; and one looking directly at the snowman. This allowed George to look at the snowman as he was being built and even make some comments on the user's choices.

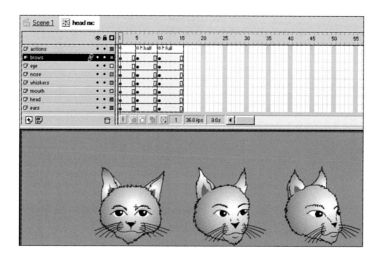

Figure 2.6 *The three heads of George.*

We developed a Movie Clip that contained George's head in the three states. Each keyframe was labeled to reflect the state. This allowed us simply to tell this Movie Clip to forward to the appropriate frame label whenever we wanted to change George's profile. I will talk about this in a minute. First, I want to quickly discuss George's eyes, ears, nose, whiskers, and mouth.

George's nose and ears did not animate, and required that we simply develop three different versions of each for the three different profiles of George. All these drawings and modifications were done directly in Flash.

The whiskers were just a simple Movie Clip containing ten individual whisker lines with two states: moving and static. The moving state is just a simple tween animation that loops until we tell it to return to the static state. Because whiskers are just lines, we did not have to create individual versions for the three head states—we simply transformed the same Movie Clip to match the perspective we wanted. This saved us both time and file size. This would not be the same case for the eyes.

The eyes for George were a combination of pupils, corneas, eyelids, eyebrows, and other small elements. We wanted to create various expressions depending on what selections the user made and do this in all three of the head perspectives. It was really quite easy.

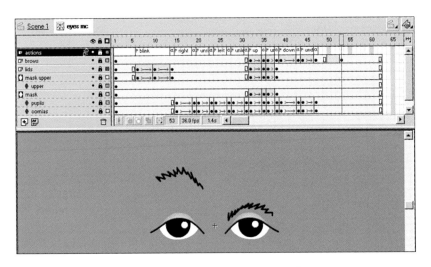

Figure 2.7   *Jeepers, creepers, where'd you get those peepers?*

Our first step was to create an individual layer for each element of the eye. We then identified six states we wanted for the straight-on view: looking straight ahead, looking left, looking right, looking up, looking down, and also raising an eyebrow for a quizzical expression. Again, we labeled each state we could to call out from the main timeline to change George's expression at will. For the eye movements, we simply created a series of shape and motion tweens.

Our next steps involved duplicating these same efforts for the half and side states of George's head. We had hoped we could utilize many of the same elements from the main eyes as we did with the whiskers, but we quickly learned that simple transformations to the eyes did not match perspective. Instead, it gave George a demented look and forced us to create individual eyes.

Teaching George to Talk

George is a rare bread of cat: He can talk. One of the keys to his success as a marketing device was his personality. On the TV commercials, George's mouth didn't move—you just heard his voice. His voice was very distinguished and added a lot to his personality. We needed to make sure we captured this in the Web site and the viral marketing campaign. Because the viral marketing campaign would eventually be attached to an e-mail or downloaded from the Web, we didn't want to add the weight of narrative audio. The file would have been huge.

Without a voice, George loses a great deal of his personality. To compensate for this, we decided to have his mouth move when he was saying something. As you can see in Figure 2.8, George's words appeared in an old familiar cartoon device known as a *bubble*.

Had we used audio for George's voice, we would have wanted to synchronize his mouth movements to match the various pronunciations of the words as he spoke them. This would have required much more effort than the timeframe allowed. First, we would need to create many different shapes for his mouth. Then we would need to step through the narration and match up the mouth movements with the appropriate pronunciations. Luckily for us, the user would most likely be reading the text in the bubble instead of reading George's lips, so we had to implement only a simple mouth Movie Clip of his lips moving up and down.

Figure 2.8 *Hey look, a talking cat!*

After some experimentation and tweaking, we got lucky and were able to transform a single mouth MC for each of the three head states.

Tying It All Together

The first step in bringing it all together was to give each Movie Clip in George's head an instance name; for example, we called the eye Movie Clips eyes and eyes 2. Back in the main George Movie Clip, we simply created a series of states and called out to the necessary action desired. If we wanted to show George not talking, we would arrange a series of eye, mouth, and head combinations and call the frame where they all resided quiet. The quiet state of George could then be called from anywhere in the movie and George would perform the necessary actions.

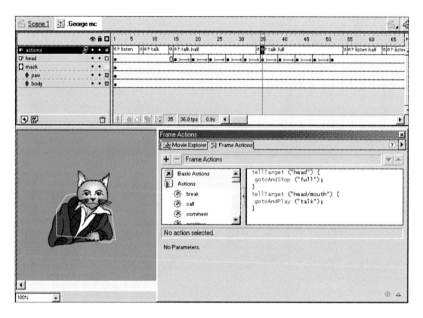

Figure 2.9 *George timeline.*

For example, we wanted George to look at the snowman and talk when the user selected an item (such as a hat). We had a frame labeled `talk full` that contained the following combination of frame actions that we required for George to look at the snowman and talk. The frame action was as follows:

```
tellTarget ("head") {
    gotoAndStop ("full");
}
tellTarget ("head/mouth") {
    gotoAndPlay ("talk");
}
```

I would like to mention that this example is a Flash 4 solution and utilizes some deprecated syntax such as the `tellTarget` action. It still works in Flash 5 and is a very simple solution. It is also a very cost-effective and efficient means to develop a project if you are under a *tight budget and timeframe. The goal of this book is not to turn you into an ActionScripting master, but instead to talk about real client projects, some of the challenges we encountered, and to show you how we overcame obstacles such as small budgets or tight timeframes with effective Flash solutions. Later chapters will cover more advanced techniques in Flash 5.*

By creating a series of frame labels and actions for every possible movement George could make, we had an efficient yet simple way to tell George how to move depending on the user's action. Here's another example: If we want George to wait on the user, we would call a frame labeled listen that had the following actions telling George to look at the user and—basically—to shut up.

```
tellTarget ("head") {
    gotoAndStop (1);
}
tellTarget ("head/mouth") {
    gotoAndStop (1);
}
stop ();
```

In the next section, I will talk about the ActionScripting that calls out to George's head and tells it what to do.

Dressing the Snowman

For users to truly enjoy the game and pass it along to their friends, it had to be very simple yet maintain a certain level of entertainment. It also had to have more than a few combinations and yet be easy enough for users of all ages to enjoy. We explored a variety of ideas, including a couch invaders game in which the user had to shoot falling items from the sky with a cleaning spray bottle before they landed on the couch and stained it. (Later on, we did develop this game—never throw out a good idea.) With the holidays fast approaching, we decided to develop a puzzle that allowed users to dress their own snowman.

The original concept involved George heckling users when they made the wrong choices; only when they chose the right combination of elements did they win and receive a coupon for a discount on their next purchase. A small focus group that we conducted determined that users didn't care so much about receiving a coupon as they did about completing the snowman the way they wanted to. So, we removed the puzzle component and allowed the users to create any kind of snowman they wanted. This is a good example of going into a project with the flexibility needed to evolve the concept into something better. It also was smart of us to take the time and conduct an evaluation of the idea using a focus group. We often get so convinced that our idea is the best that the final solution misses the mark. Conducting a focus group can seem like a distraction, but it always pays off in the end if only to prove your idea is great!

We then came up with the idea of letting the user create a holiday card with a picture of their newly created snowman that they could e-mail to friends. The plan was to implement Generator for the creation of the cards. However, the short timeframe and the fact that Generator was not yet compatible with Flash 4 ruled this option out as well. We later found out that we made all the right choices because what users really wanted to do was simply to be able to create their own snowman and to let friends enjoy building their own snowmen as well. This sharing with others provided the viral component.

So, it was now time to create a variety of elements such as eyes, hats, and accessories. In some cases, we developed themes such as the cowboy, the clown, and Darth Maul from *Star Wars Episode I: The Phantom Menace*. Others are just crazy costume pieces that we had fun creating.

Figure 2.10   *The cowboy snowman.*

The early pieces included a cigar for the gangster and gave the cowboy a gun that fired. Furniture.com marketing immediately axed these and made sure that we had nonviolent and uncontroversial characters and props. The lasso replaced the gun and the festive horn blower replaced the cigar.

After each of the elements was approved by the client and drawn in Flash, we created individual Movie Clips for each. Because they were originally created on the snowman, we avoided any later issues with pieces looking awkward.

In some cases, we created simple animations such as the lasso twirling or the rubber chicken being tossed in the air. These animations were simple shape and motion tweens and required the snowman's right arm to animate as well. By making sure that each of the accessory animations shared the same arm, we saved ourselves some extra work as well as minimized the overall file size.

Figure 2.11 *The extreme snowman.*

Adding User Controls

At this point in the game, the project plan had been approved—including the overall design, the interactivity, the animation, and the comments that George would make. It was now time to wire it all together and implement the functionality.

Figure 2.12   *The Darth Maul snowman.*

We identified seven snowman elements that the user could control: hat, eyes, nose, mouth, neck, front, and accessory. In addition to these interactive components, the text bubble that displays George's comments above his head needed to be wired in to the final solution.

We first created each accessory as a Movie Clip directly on the snowman to ensure that it would fit exactly. Then, for each group of snowman elements (hats, eyes, and so on), we created one Movie Clip that contained all nine possible accessories. Each possibility was placed in a different labeled keyframe and each one had exactly the same center point so that it would appear in the correct place on the snowman.

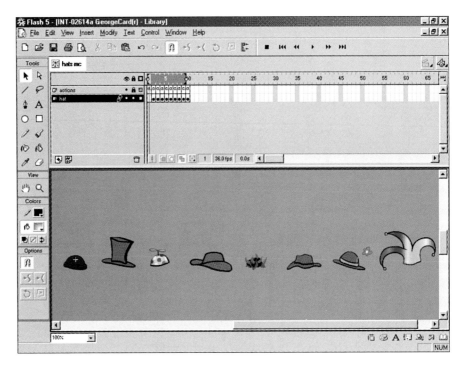

Figure 2.13   *The snowman's hat collection.*

For example, the Hat Movie Clip had nine frames, one for each hat. On each frame, we placed a `stop` frame action. We then placed a blank keyframe at the beginning of the hat Movie Clip and placed an instance of this Movie Clip on the main timeline on the snowman's head. Finally, we gave it an instance name of Movie Clip `hat` and repeated this entire process for the eyes, the nose, and the remaining elements including the text bubble.

This simple plan allowed us to add code to a button that calls to the appropriate Movie Clip and tells it which hat to display. Nothing fancy required.

Figure 2.14   *All the empty elements on the snowman. Also known as the naked truth.*

The next step was to create the buttons that allow the user to select the various snowman accessories. We called this the *button panel*. The button panel is a simple Movie Clip that vertically lists all the user's choices: hat, eyes, mouth, and so on. Note that this symbol is not a button but a Movie Clip. The buttons are found inside the Movie Clip, on the text for each of the elements. By building it this way, we can have one simple Movie Clip that expands to display the various accessories available for each group.

Figure 2.15 shows the first few frames of the button panel, which contain the collapsed state. When the user rolls over any of the text buttons, a highlight appears. When the user clicks on one of the text buttons, it moves the button panel timeline to the appropriately labeled frame: eyes, mouth, and so on. At these frames, the panel expands to show the various choices to the user.

You should notice that each element is on its own layer. For example, the main button panel text buttons are on one layer and the contents of the expanded button panel are located on another. This is an efficient design because it requires each of the elements to be loaded only once and maximizes the feedback time of the button to the user.

Each button panel instance contains nine selections for each element: nine hats, nine eyes, and so on. Each

selectable accessory is a unique button and that is where
the Actions are initialized.

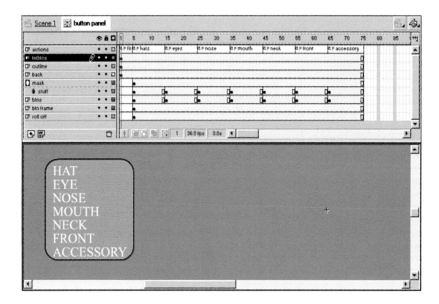

Figure 2.15   *All that in the timeline for just a button?*

Let's step back and retrace our steps. The user rolls over
the button panel Movie Clip and rests over the eyes button
Movie Clip. The eyes button has a frame action that says:

```
on (release) {
    gotoAndStop ("eyes");
}
```

When the button is clicked, this script tells the button panel
Movie Clip to go to the frame labeled eyes and stop. The
button panel timeline jumps to frame label eyes and
encounters a stop frame action. At this point in the timeline,
the button panel is expanded to show the nine choices for
eyes. The user can click the other main text buttons and the
button panel timeline will jump to the corresponding frame:
mouth, hat, and so on.

Before I talk about each individual eye button, let's talk about how to collapse the expanded button panel. Directly above all the elements in the main button panel Movie Clip is a giant invisible button with the following action:

```
on (rollOver) {
    gotoAndStop ("first");
}
```

This simple solution resets the button panel to its original collapsed state if the user rolls off the button panel choices.

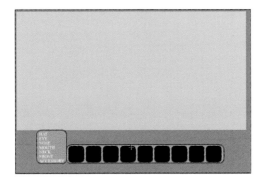

Figure 2.16   *Invisible buttons are clearly a simple solution.*

Finally, I need to cover the actions for the individual accessory buttons. For each group in the expanded button panel there are nine choices. Behind each choice is an invisible button. If the user clicks the third eye selection, the following actions take place:

```
on (release) {
    tellTarget ("/eyes") {
        gotoAndStop (4);
    }
    tellTarget ("/speech") {
        gotoAndPlay ("neg7");
    }
}
```

This simple code says, on release tell the target "/eyes"—meaning the Movie Clip on the main timeline with the instance name of eyes—to go to frame 4 and stop. Frame 4 of eyes contains the Movie Clip that corresponds to the eyes the user clicked. The script then goes on to tell the Movie Clip speech on the main timeline to go to frame neg7 and play. This displays the correct text for George to say and moves his mouth.

Keep in mind that this is using a relative targeting method with the slash syntax. The slash syntax has been deprecated in Flash 5 although it will still work. Should we ever need to work on this project again (which is unlikely because Furniture.com is out of business) or had we developed this solution when Flash 5 was available, we would use the following code, which produces the same results:

```
on (release) {
    with (_root.eyes) {
        gotoAndStop (4);
    }
    with (_root.speech) {
        gotoAndPlay ("neg7");
    }
}
```

It is a good practice to get comfortable with the new Flash 5 ActionScripting syntax. In the Actions panel, you can tell Flash to highlight those actions that have been deprecated.

For George's comments, we built a Movie Clip with approximately twenty different comments George might make, such as "You sure you want to do that?" and "Howdy Partner" if the user selects one of the cowboy items. Remember, George is a bit pompous and has some attitude. We labeled each frame according to the comment George makes and simply call out from each button pressed one comment that we think is appropriate.

In addition to the frame label for each comment, we have a simple action that tells George to move his head to one of the various states: straight on, half, or full side:

```
tellTarget ("/george") {
    gotoAndPlay ("talk half");
}
```

These extremely simple button actions, when combined with frame actions and simple animations, allowed the user to take control of the puzzle and have fun. They allowed us to develop a solution in a very short period of time. But we weren't done yet.

Final Touches

We wanted to create an immersive experience; that is, we wanted our little game to put the user in the holiday spirit. To accomplish this, we started with a nice wintry scene of George's house surrounded by snowdrifts and snow-covered trees. The cartoon style of the drawings mixed with our jazzy holiday music loop to set the mood nicely. The glowing candles in the windows and the simple shape tweens for the chimney smoke added to the effect as well.

Early in the main timeline, this frame action tells the music to start playing:

```
tellTarget ("/music") {
    gotoAndStop ("music");
}
```

We also created a simple holiday bell button that allowed the user to toggle the music on and off. Typically, we do not believe in over-repetitive audio loops because they can be irritating, so we always give an audio off switch. As a side note, this loop worked rather nicely and was well received by our test group.

For the audio toggle, we simply created a Movie Clip with two frames. The first frame has a stop action in it and the bell button indicates that the music is playing. On the bell button, we include the following button action:

```
on (release) {
    stopAllSounds ();
    tellTarget ("/music") {
        gotoAndStop (1);
    }
    nextFrame ();
}
```

This simply tells the music to stop playing and then sends the bell Movie Clip to the next frame. On that frame, it encounters a stop action and displays the bell button in a state indicating that the music is no longer playing. If the user clicks on the button, the following script is activated that tells the music to start up again:

```
on (release) {
    tellTarget ("/music") {
        gotoAndPlay ("music");
    }
    prevFrame ();
}
```

Again, a simple solution for a simple project. There is no need to reinvent the wheel or make the project more complex than it needs to be. This is particularly true when you are dealing with real clients, real budgets, and real timeframes.

Other nice touches that we were able to implement easily because of Flash include the transparency of the glass window behind George. Flash doesn't have the most intuitive color-mixing environment, but it is capable of producing the results you need for most instances. In this case, we simply created a new radial gradient with white and a light blue. We gave both colors an alpha setting of 50%, which made them semi-transparent. Another way we could have done this was by creating a symbol for just the glass, using opaque colors, and then applying an alpha effect to the entire glass symbol. Either works just as well.

Figure 2.17   *It sure looks cozy inside.*

Other touches we added that polished the piece up nicely include the fade to night after the user indicates he is done. Applying a tint effect to all the elements creates this simple effect. By keeping the candles on a higher layer and applying no effect, they really stand out and create a warm and cozy feel.

We also included glittering stars, which are just a duplication and resizing of one simple star symbol that we have fade in and out. A similar simple technique is applied to the falling snow. Only one flake is used repetitively, but we have many instances of it following a series of individual guide layers. This effect is quite subtle but effective.

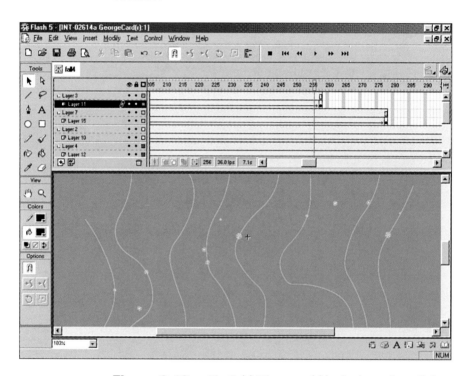

Figure 2.18 *Mr. Cold Miser would be jealous. Snowflakes following motion guides.*

As this project was being developed, Furniture.com was going through an identity rebranding process; that is, it was creating a new logo.

This new logo includes a lamp and a light effect against a dark background. Because we were fading to a night scene at the end of the project, we had some fun with the logo. Instead of having the logo appear static with the light on, which most users would never notice, we had the light switch on a couple of seconds after the night transitions in.

The light from the lamp would also illuminate the lampshade and the .com in the logo. Not only was this fun, but it also attracted the user's eye and encouraged him to click on the logo, which launched a browser and took the user to Furniture.com's site, where he received a coupon.

To implement the link from the logo, we told the text to act as a button with the following action:

```
on (release) {
    getURL ("http://www.furniture.com", "_blank");
}
```

This simply says put the Furniture.com URL into a new browser window. The user's computer recognizes the HTTP protocol request from the Flash piece and knows to launch a browser. This simple code is utilized several times within the piece.

E-mail Marketing

A new experience for me on this project was the use of outsourced e-mail services. The service works like this: Furniture.com provides the e-mail marketing firm with a list of e-mail addresses the company would like to market to. We provide them with a message and the George application we just finished. The e-mail marketing company then e-mails the message and the application to every person on the list. Sounds simple, right? Why wouldn't Furniture.com do this on its own?

The reason is the same as why most of us pay to have our oil changed instead of doing it ourselves. It is quicker, more convenient, and worth the few extra dollars to have someone else do it for us. And we get extra services.

First is the sheer massive size of the e-mailing. A typical Furniture.com customer list exceeded 100,000 names. Sending this number of e-mails would crush a typical company's server. In addition, the e-mail service handles all delivery errors and outdated e-mail accounts. It also sends the e-mail during the wee hours of the night so that most people would get the e-mail first thing in the morning. Then, the service analyzes and tracks results, provides reports, and most importantly, it handled what are called *opt outs*.

For those of you not familiar with the term, *opt in* and *opt out marketing* refers to giving the end user the choice of opting in or out of an e-mail marketing program. If you've ever bought anything online or filled out a form for information, you've probably seen a small question at the end that asks you to check the box if you want to receive a newsletter or be on a mailing list to receive special offers, and so on. If the question asks you to check the box not to receive these offers, this is called *opting out*. If the message asks you to check the box to be included in the notifications, this is called *opting in*.

It's a rather simple concept that is the center of many debates about which type is politically correct and which type violates the rights of online consumers.

No matter which method a company employs, federal law requires companies to provide the consumer with the ability to unsubscribe or opt out of any lists. The benefit of having an e-mail marketing service handle your large list e-mailing needs is that it can handle all those users who want to opt out and ensure that they do not receive any more contacts. Nothing upsets a customer more than when he asks to not be on your mailing list and you continue to send him e-mails.

You Should See a Doctor About That Virus

A scary moment happened the day after we e-mailed the puzzle when we discovered that our viral marketing campaign contained a virus. No pun intended, we sent more than 100,000 people a George the Cat game that contained a virus! Or so we thought. It turns out that Norton antivirus software listed Flash-generated .exe files as a trojan horse.

A *trojan horse* is a file that masquerades as a helpful program, but turns out to be a program that does harm to your computer. There was nothing wrong with our file; Norton just needed to update its list so that our file was not identified as a virus, which happened the next day. Talk about being scared! The press would have had a field day with this type of news.

Post-Mortem

When all was said and done, the project proved to be wildly successful. The response rate to the e-mails was something like 20% (which is outstanding) and approximately 5,000 new customers were acquired because of this campaign. The per-customer acquisition cost—meaning the entire cost of the marketing effort divided by the number of new customers gained—was significantly lower than any other Furniture.com marketing effort to date.

If we had an opportunity to do things differently, I would like to have better navigational controls, smooth out the full-screen transitions, and even utilize Macromedia Generator to offer dynamic coupons in real time and allow users to forward personalized cards to their friends.

I think the project could be better optimized to reduce bandwidth as well. With Flash 5 and MP3 compression, we could have easily saved more than 100KB. Some of the shapes could be better optimized, particularly the candles, snowflakes, and cottage.

All in all, it was an excellent project. We worked hard for ten days, but provided the client with an excellent solution at a cost-effective price.

CHAPTER

DesignMentor.com

INTERMEDIATE

An entire site in Flash.

Overview

Flash can be used for much more than just animations and presentations or elements of a site. Flash can be the entire Web site. This chapter will follow the DesignMentor.com project from start to finish as we develop from scratch a Web site that's standard and full-featured using nothing but Flash and a little HTML. We will look at how we pitched the client and will closely examine the 3D elements used on the final solution. We will also discuss the transitions from concept to model to Flash. If you have never built an entire site in Flash, this chapter will give you a glimpse into what you can expect, how to sell the idea to the client, and some of the necessary elements you need to consider before the solution is Web ready.

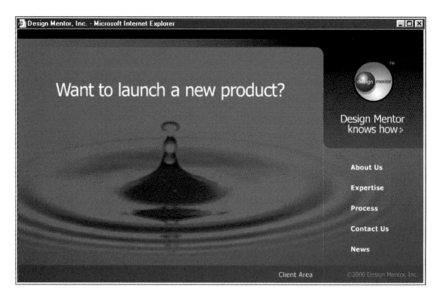

Figure 3.1 *The final solution.*

The Players

Throughout my career, I have held many jobs and many different titles. At one point or another over the past five years, Flash became a part of what I did. Whether I was working as an employee, freelance, or as the owner of my own company, part of my job has always been to identify new opportunities.

One night my wife told me that we were going out to dinner with a new friend and her husband, and we would be meeting at this great little restaurant in Manchester, NH. It was an early summer night and particularly warm out, so we chose a table outside where we could see the city walking by and enjoy the nice weather.

We arrived early and found my wife's friend waiting for us. She told us that her husband would be joining us shortly and apologized because he was coming straight from work and would be wearing shorts. My first thought was "Why would you apologize for that?" My second thought was "That's pretty cool—he can wear shorts at work." I knew from conversations with my wife that they were successful, but I had no idea what business he was in other than something to do with engineering.

Of course, I imagined your typical stereotype engineer with a pocket protector, glasses, and conservative personality.

Sorry, Doug! I should note that this really isn't what Doug is like, but on first appearances, it's hard to tell.

I came to find out Doug Vincent is the founder and CEO of Design Mentor, a medical product engineering company started about a year before this meeting. Design Mentor consists of mechanical, software, and human engineers that specialize in developing medical pumps and devices that clean fluids such as blood. Their clients are primarily extremely large medical manufacturing companies. It is a very unique company with some exceptional people.

At this point in dinner, Doug and I hadn't said much other than a few jokes while the wives went on and on about their teams (they're both coaches and that's how they met). Sooner or later, the wives gave us a chance to jump into the conversation and Doug asked what I do for work. I had just recently left Furniture.com and was interviewing with companies, working on my golf handicap, and in the middle of one medium-sized Flash project for a company owned by a friend of mine.

The job interviewing was going extremely well because this was still the peak of the dot-com craze and the headhunters had caught wind that I was on the market. I had more offers and interviews than I could ever want. The strange thing is that no matter how good the offer was, something kept telling me to hold back, to wait. What I was waiting for, I wasn't sure.

Through an executive search firm in Boston, I learned about this venture capital–owned small business located within a short distance from my home. Until now I had spent my career commuting from the beautiful southern New Hampshire area to Boston and the surrounding Rt. 128 technology loop. The prospect of having a 15-minute commute alone was tempting. This company was looking for someone with my experience to take a significant ownership in the business as CEO and build the business to compete with the Boston market. Despite the incredible compensation plan, something was telling me it wasn't the right choice for me.

I knew that at this point in my career offers wouldn't get much better, so I began to examine what could be causing these hesitations. At the time, I barely understood that it was a desire to start my own company that was keeping me from going to work for anyone else. Someday I will hope no one reads this book, and I will tell everyone that I knew from the day I was born that I was driven to launch my own company, but the reality is different.

So, I was explaining to Doug that I had not yet identified the company that I wanted to work for and was considering starting my own business. Little did I know that this dinner would be the night I decided to stop interviewing and focus on the creation of my own company, Hookumu.

Figure 3.2 *The Hookumu logo that hadn't even been designed yet.*

Doug immediately became interested because he had known for years that he wanted to start his own company and just a year earlier founded Design Mentor Incorporated. He began to ask all sorts of questions about my business and my idea, and mentioned the fact that Design Mentor was currently conducting a search for a Web development firm to build its next Web site. At the time, I wasn't extremely excited about the prospect of building a static HTML Web site.

Nonetheless, I was very excited about the prospect of landing a new client and taking on another project when no one—even my wife, at that point—knew I would no longer be looking to other companies for a job.

The Client's Need: Introducing DesignMentor.com

Figure 3.3   *The Design Mentor identity.*

So, this time I found myself sitting in the kitchen of the home of Design Mentor's co-founder, Brian Key. Typical of companies started from grass roots and not venture capital funding, the Design Mentor office is Brian's house. They did an amazing job of routing a network through the various rooms and even converting the finished basement into a full functioning lab for testing purposes. It was very cool. (You should see the new office building they have built since then, wow.) So Brian, Doug, and myself are sitting around a granite-countered kitchen island with laptops out, discussing each other's capabilities and needs and trying to see whether there is a fit between our two organizations.

The company's current site was a typical first Web site for a small company founded in the late 1990s. It was built entirely in HTML and had the logo at the top and navigation down the left side. The design was some abstract shape that had no relevance to Design Mentor's industry or capabilities.

It seems that Design Mentor's clients would commit to large contracts and when the client or client's CFO went to the site, they would question the stability of the organization. This was a classic example of a Web site doing harm to a company's capability to win and conduct business. After a basic discovery meeting, it was determined that Design Mentor's greatest need for a Web site was to communicate the company's unique approach and to appear worthy of the million-dollar contracts that it was asking its clients to commit to. After all, Design Mentor had a phenomenal team with exceptional experience and credentials. There was no weakness in its business other than its Web site. The company was on the verge of a growth phase and the site needed to more accurately reflect the business.

The Solution

Initially the plan never involved Flash. I started the project, as I do most site development projects, with a discovery phase in which I interviewed, questioned, and documented every facet of the business. This is a standard approach that has proven to be very effective on most projects. I capture all the information in a formatted Microsoft Word document that I later use to confirm our findings with the client. Eventually it's included in the final proposal.

Not only does this help me keep all the information in a central location, but it also helps avoid potential pitfalls later in the project. By submitting all my findings and the project plan for client approval early in the project, it is very easy to identify later on whether issues or requests are new or were part of the original request.

When complete, the discovery documents tend to be approximately twenty pages long and typically contain a similar format depending on the type of project. During the discovery phase and thereafter, I post the document online for all project members—including the clients—to collaborate on, add to, and modify. This is a good practice to undertake with your projects even if it's just an e-mail message you pass back and forth. Some of my discovery documents are a single page and others grow into hundreds of pages. It is not the size that matters—insert joke here—but the simple idea that you track all of the details of the project in one accessible location.

For this project, the discovery document contained information about the company such as its unique attributes, employees, who its clients were, what types of services the company offered, who its competition was. It also included more tactical information such as how the company intended to manage site content after the launch, what type of computer systems its users owned, and the basic deadline and budget of the project.

With all this information, it was relatively easy for myself to develop a project plan that met all the new site requirements. In this case, we were talking about primarily a brochure Web site. This basically means the client was not looking to facilitate client communications, conduct e-commerce transactions, implement communications with back-end accounting systems or develop a portal. The company simply wanted to have a professional-looking site that reflected the company's unique strengths and appeared as strong and capable online as it was offline.

It was clear early on there wouldn't be a great deal of content and that there was no need for any type of database platform. At this point, I started to lose a little excitement in the project. I knew it didn't make sense to

89

suggest a robust content management platform, and that the pages would be mostly static data. The site would be simple no matter what technology I suggested and started thinking that HTML was the best solution.

I wanted the site to be engaging and something I could showcase. That would be difficult to do with minimal static content and HTML. At first, the client and I started playing with the idea of many embedded Flash movies inside the various HTML pages. This started to get interesting, but we were concerned about the impact the growing complexity would have on the project. After all, the client is our first concern; I didn't want to pitch a solution that would be twice the cost of what Design Mentor needed and also would be expensive to update and maintain.

At this point, I started considering an entire site developed in Flash. I'd seen it done before, but only with a handful of sites and most of those for design firms. I set out to see whether any other companies had made this commitment and was stunned to see Tiffany & Co. jewelers was offering its entire Web site in Flash. I was thrilled.

The best Flash Web sites I was familiar with were stunningly beautiful, interactive, and required tremendous talent to build, but none was built for commercial purposes (or for actual clients, for that matter). Most of these sites were experiments, Web sites for interactive development firms, or for very targeted audiences. At this point in my career, I'd developed several Flash-based sites for clients such as JAMN 94.5 (a Boston-area radio station), Lotus Development Corporation, and other primarily leading-edge organizations.

To create a Flash-based Web site for a young, relatively unknown engineering company whose clients would be executives at very large medical manufacturing corporations, potential product engineers looking for jobs, and managers wanting to monitor their projects was uncharted terrain. I was also concerned that building such a site, although very exciting for Hookumu, would not be a successful solution for the client. After all, that is what this book is about: creating successful real world e-commerce solutions.

I had a vision. I was confident that I could succeed, and more importantly, I knew it could be a success for the client. If Tiffany's could develop a Flash-based e-commerce solution to market and sell jewelry, I knew I had the correct approach for an engineering company with leading edge services.

To help close the deal with the client, I put together a solid proposal. The proposal included a plan to develop an information architecture (IA) for the new site before any development began. I expect most of you know what an information architecture is, but often our clients do not. An *information architecture* is an overall diagram of the Web site. It is not a sitemap that shows every link in the site, but a 50,000 foot view of the Web site and the various "buckets" of information. To help communicate what an information architecture is, I usually include an IA of the client's current site in the proposal. As long as the site is not extremely large, it helps to illustrate what it is with a minimal time investment. If it's a large site, I show examples from other projects and then include billable time to architect the current site. This helps me become familiar with the current site and allows me to work quickly with the client to identify those areas that are valuable in the current design. If the clients aren't familiar with their own site—and some clients aren't—they can easily step through the site with the IA at their side. Figures 3.4 and 3.5 show the before and after information architectures for the DesignMentor.com site.

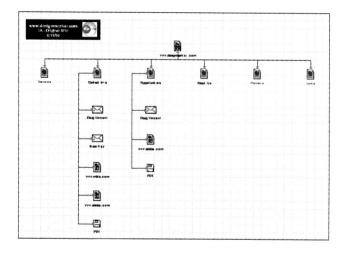

Figure 3.4 *The original DesignMentor.com Information Architecture; not a very robust site.*

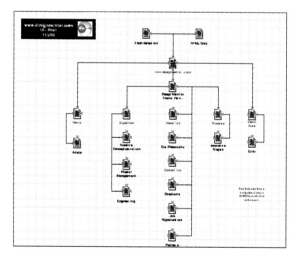

Figure 3.5 *After many meetings and much planning, the new DesignMentor.com information architecture.*

Ultimately, the client chose Hookumu because of many factors but the one element that closed the deal was stating that my goal with DesignMentor.com was to develop an award-winning site that I could showcase in our Hookumu.com gallery. The client was really drawn to this statement. Making this statement inherits a certain level of risk. I typically prefer not to set the clients expectations so high because then it's far easier to let them down. Instead, I prefer to be realistic and then exceed the client's expectations. However, in this case, because I'd just started out, I knew that I wouldn't let this project be anything but a success.

> *Be very careful. Many firms have established poor reputations in the Internet market by over-promising and under-delivering. It is far better for your business to under-promise and over-deliver.*

Upon presentation of the project plan and suggestion of the Flash Web site, I was excited to learn that the client was very flexible and had the faith in my abilities to allow me to experiment and learn that Flash can be an effective Web site medium. It was now time to deliver.

Plan It First: Interaction Model

With the discovery sessions largely complete and the information architecture nearly approved, I took another step to plan before I built: developing an interaction model. This is an over-used term that could have different meanings from company to company. For Hookumu, an *interaction model* is the process of visually representing the various elements that will be on every screen of the Web site, including buttons, links, and so on.

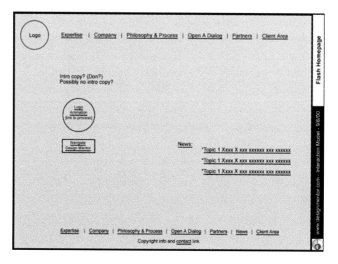

Figure 3.6 *Scene from the interaction model.*

Although this deliverable is a visual layout of each scene, no graphic design or artwork has been started yet. I'm not even suggesting that any thought has been given to the position of the elements on each screen. The single goal of the interaction model is to represent every element that each page, or page template, will have. This is a time-consuming but very effective tool to utilize in the Web site development process.

An interaction model allows your developers, designers, and the client to agree on what is being built before any time is spent building it. After it is approved, the entire team can proceed with a clear understanding of each page's features and functionality. It's far easier to build against an approved spec than it is to continually add features, functionality, and elements as the design and code are being developed. One metaphor I often use is that if you were building a house, you wouldn't make decisions about how big you want the foundation to be while the builders are shingling the roof. Technically, you could do it, but not only would the builders hate you, you also would spend a fortune tearing down the completed work and the end product would never be as clean as if you had started from scratch with the proper plan.

Plan the Design: Rounds

Artwork is subjective and can be difficult to estimate. I've seen artists create some of the best Web designs only to have the client butcher it in a design review. Building a profitable business model around anything creative can be a challenge and a risk. To offset this risk, we have refined a process we call *rounds*.

For Web design in our first round, I present the client with three to five designs in black-and-white. Typically, I present all-around designs as GIFs and JPEGs in a Web page. This allows the clients to review the designs before or after the meeting at their leisure. First, I quickly skim through thumbnails of the five designs. This allows the client to get a brief look at what is coming, kind of like a movie trailer. I have learned that if you just start showing the designs one at a time, clients can have a hard time focusing on the current design while they anticipate the next one. By quickly showing all five designs, the clients know what to expect.

I then go through each black-and-white design in full size. The purpose for black-and-white, and not color, is that clients can easily be distracted by a dominating color and like or hate a particular design regardless of whether it is a good or a bad design. I also explain to the client that there is only a slim chance that one of the designs will be perfect and that perfection was not my goal. In the first round, my goal is to present the client with five very different styles and artistic directions. One design might have a dark background and another a white background. One design might be boxed in tightly and another has no boundaries— you get the picture. What I hope to achieve is very specific feedback from each black-and-white design.

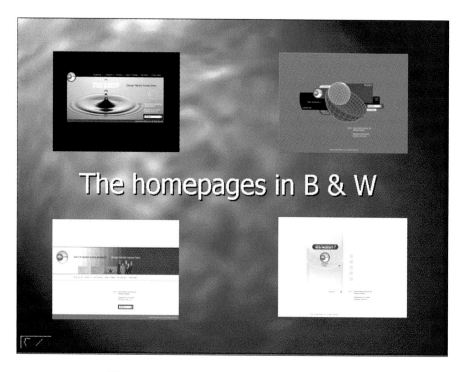

Figure 3.7 *Thumbnail designs.*

I then show each of the designs in full color. It always amazes me how people will quickly change the design they like based on the addition of color. I am a firm believer that it needs to look good in black-and-white before it can ever look good in color. Color has such a powerful impact. As I walk through each design in color, I gather all comments and feedback from everyone. Armed with all this information, I can go away and pick two or three specific creative paths to explore.

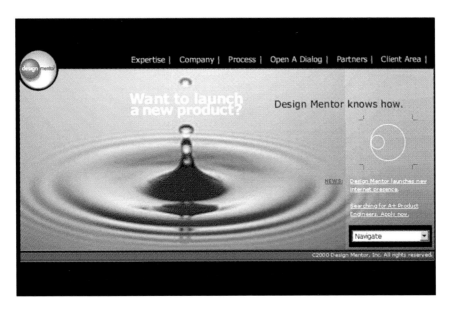

Figure 3.8   *Round 1 design exploring the use of a single dominant image.*

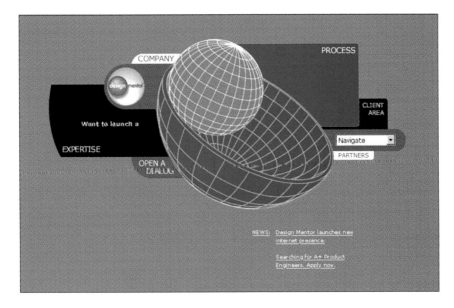

Figure 3.9   *Round 1 design exploring the play on the engineering aspect with modular shapes and no bounding boxes.*

Figure 3.10 *Round 1 design exploring the corporate approach through the use of clean and cold colors.*

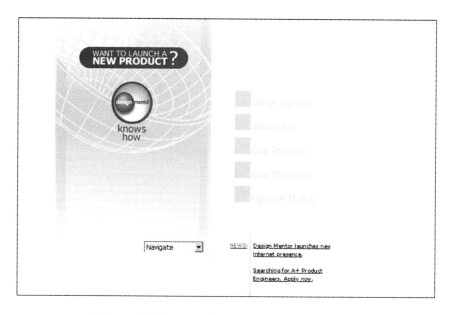

Figure 3.11 *Another Round 1 design taking the corporate approach, but this time with few boundaries and a nontraditional layout.*

On a project of this size, I like to have three rounds. Four or five designs are presented for round 1 and three designs with subpages are presented for round 2. Finally, in round 3, I present one homepage design with three or four subpages. This approach involves the client in the design evolution of the site and greatly reduces the risk of having to go back to the drawing board at any stage in the game.

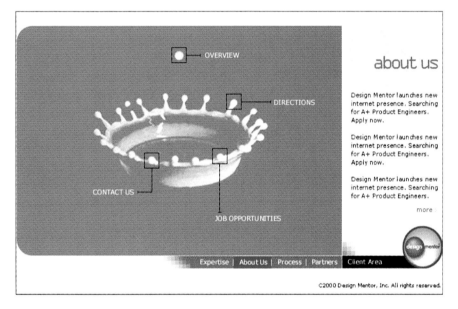

Figure 3.12   *This round 2 design is based on specific feedback from the client regarding the exploration of the water drop theme.*

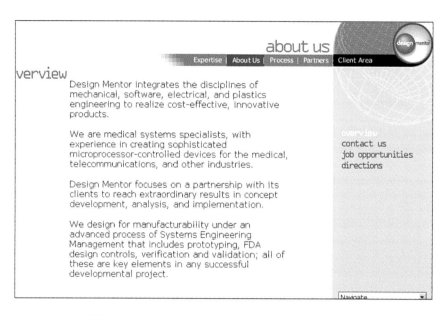

Figure 3.13   *A round 2 design indicating how a subpage would look with a lot of body copy.*

Figure 3.14   *This round 2 design shows further evolution of the homepage after implementing suggestions from the client.*

Figure 3.15   *A round 2 subpage showing how navigation devices would look when the user interacts with them.*

I Love It when a Plan Comes Together

Enough about the process; let's talk about the thinking behind the designs. Design Mentor specializes in engineering medical products that clean fluids, such as blood. Of course, we didn't want to show blood because it typically has negative connotations. Anyone remember the movie *Carrie*?

I also didn't want to have literal imagery (showing exactly what Design Mentor does) because Design Mentor is a unique company and it would be difficult to communicate all this. What I did want was a clean, elegant design that has a visual understatement. A unique philosophy Design Mentor takes is to understate what its capabilities are. With this approach, they set the expectations of the client low and then exceed them with the final deliverable. This is not to say that Design Mentor doesn't correctly communicate what they undersell, they just don't parade around indicating how great they are. It's a unique approach that has a very positive effect on clients. We wanted to reflect this philosophy in the designs.

Of the three initial designs, the team immediately gravitated to the water drop. Some of you might be familiar with Dr. Edgerton, the scientist who took high-speed still photography of milk drops splashing and bullets ripping through apples.

This had great appeal to the client due to this relationship of liquids and fluids and science and research. It also had the understatement effect I was looking to reflect. The design was professionally designed yet did not scream at you. I spent a great deal of time in Photoshop revising and cleaning up the drop to get the feel I was looking for. Because Hookumu doesn't have high-speed photography equipment like Dr. Edgerton did, I used stock photography. The original image was on a white background with a color gradient from top to bottom. Because I would be showing the image so large, the touch-ups had to be perfect.

Figure 3.16 *Drip-drip.*

For the subpages, I explored using a unique image for each separate area of the site. I created some designs that included Dr. Edgerton's crown splash photograph. Although it was engaging, it did not have the same power of the single drop, and some people mistook it for a king's crown. I also tried an image of a crewing boat leaving the scene with a wake behind it but it wasn't quite right either. I started to learn that the power in the homepage design was the simplicity of the it and the lack of many elements.

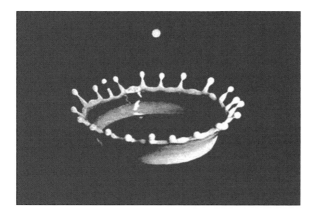

Figure 3.17   *Got milk? Crown drip-drip.*

Other images quickly became weakened when I was forced to place fields of color over them to incorporate the body text. In the end, only the homepage imagery seemed to work because the viewers weren't left guessing what the image was, they already knew. Instead, I decided to use color-coding for each of the main areas.

When I decided to color-code the various areas but use the same background image, I started to think about the best ways to do this. Although it would have been easiest to colorize the images in an exterior application such as Photoshop and bring in unique JPEGs for each, this would have made the Flash file sizes huge. I managed to reduce each JPEG down to less than 6KB by the time it left Flash, but I had at least five color-coded areas and this would have been an additional 30KB with little payoff. Always conserve bandwidth and the user will thank you.

I explored applying tints and advanced effects to the bitmap symbol itself, but doing so tended to dull and wash out the subtle highlights that made the imagery stunning. So, I was forced to try other means.

The best solution, and the one utilized on the live site, was actually the simplest to implement. I created a small symbol that was nothing more than a white block. On the main timeline, I stretched the block as necessary (smaller is better) and applied a series of tints and transparency effects to get the desired results.

It took a great deal of tweaking and fine-tuning because the colors all had a saturated purple feel. I kept at it and came up with six colors the client liked. My initial intention was to use just one copy of the tint Movie Clip and give it an instance name. This would allow us to use ActionScripting to apply the color transformation as necessary.

However, I found that this slowed performance considerably as users jumped from section to section. I then used unique instances of the Movie Clip with manually applied color effects, and found that this removed the performance issues and added almost no weight to the overall file size.

I guess the lesson to be learned is to experiment and allow yourself to make bad decisions—as long as you are conscious of them and you can go back and investigate the results.

Figure 3.18 *A rainbow of fruit flavors.*

Loading External Text Files

One of the true powers of Flash is its ability to dynamically load external information. Add Generator and you can dynamically add all types of data from sources including SQL, Oracle, and so on. In Chapter 6, we will discuss Generator a bit more. Even without Generator, Flash still has an amazing amount of control over external information.

For DesignMentor.com, we wanted to let the client control the textual information in external files that the site would then load on command. The client simply has a different text file to edit for each area of the site. We put the power of content management into the hands of the client for two primary reasons. First, we wanted to make sure that the clients could quickly update their own Web site. Second, although these particular clients are quite capable of figuring out Flash, we did not want to force a new technology on them just to maintain their own site. There is a third reason: Up to this point, we weren't aware of anyone who had developed a self-contained content management system for a Flash Web site, and we wanted to be the first. To accomplish this, we created two dynamic text fields on every page that we wanted to contain external text.

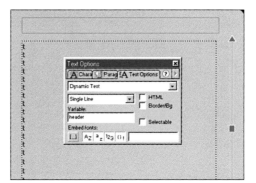

Figure 3.19   *Dynamic header.*

The first field is a single-line dynamic text field to which we assigned the variable header. The second field is a multiline dynamic text field with a variable name of Importedtext. We intentionally kept the variable names generic so that we could reuse them for any section. We could have created unique variables for each section of the site, but we would have had to develop individual dynamic text loading devices for each area.

The following frame script loads the appropriate text. This script is from the first frame of the About Us section:

```
stop ();
header = /:headAbout;
Importedtext = /:copyAbout;
tellTarget ("/tracker") {
    gotoAndPlay (1);
```

Lets walk through it. `header = /:headAbout;` tells the dynamic text field `header` to equal the variable `headAbout`. In the external text file, we tell `headAbout` to say `About Us`. Here is that exact line from the external text file:

```
headAbout=The Company
```

It's that simple. In the Flash file, we simply have one copy of the header text field and one copy of the body text field. In the frame script of each section of the site, we simply tell the dynamic field to correspond with the section the user is in. The line `header = /:headAbout;` for the About Us section is changed to `header = /:headExpertise;` for the Expertise section, and so on. The actual text that is displayed is written in the external text file. Actually, it is the client who does it. This puts the power of content management back in the hands of the client.

The reference to the body copy of each section is the next line of the frame script: `Importedtext = /:copyAbout;`. Remember `Importedtext` is the variable associated with the multiline dynamic text field for the body copy. In the external text file, we have the following:

```
&copyAbout=X
```

The character & indicates a new variable to Flash. In the earlier example, X equals all the text you want to display. In the actual text file for this page, we have many paragraphs of text. This solution is a basic one that gives the client only the ability to identify new paragraphs. This kept it simple, met the needs of the client and allowed us to avoid the complexities of developing a content management solution in Flash that gives the users full formatting control.

107

At the end of the external text file, we include the following statement: &DONE=1. DONE is a new variable that we will use later on to tell Flash that the end of the text file has been reached. More on the DONE variable in a minute.

The Pre-loader

As with all good Flash designs, we have what is typically referred to as a pre-loader. Let's quickly talk about how I ensured that everything was loaded before letting the user into the site. At this point in the project, Phil Stephenson, my ActionScripting and fast-Flash partner, jumped into the project to assist. So from now on, when I say *we*, I mean either Phil or myself.

On our main timeline, we have a Movie Clip called .trueloader stashed off the main stage out of sight. This Movie Clip is basically a series of frames that contains all the elements of the site. The elements are broken up into 10 somewhat even chunks and spread across the timeline. As each chunk of information is loaded, we tell the pre-loader to advance until finished. Here are the details.

In frame 1, we tell the site to load the About Us text into memory with the following script:

```
loadVariables ("about.txt", "/");
```

The timeline is advanced to the next keyframe and we hit:

```
if (/:DONE eq "1") {
    /:DONE = "0";
    nextFrame ();
    play ();
} else if (/:DONE ne "1") {
    prevFrame ();
    play ();
}
```

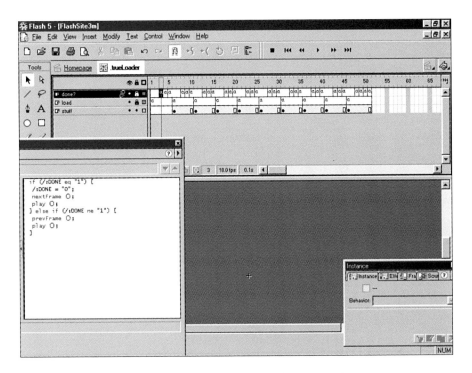

Figure 3.20 *Would the real pre-loader please stand up, please stand up.*

This `if` statement checks whether the file is completely loaded. Remember at the end of every external text file, we tell DONE to equal 1. So, if the variable DONE equals 1, that means the file is done loading, and the next line resets the variable DONE back to 0 and advances the timeline of the Movie Clip. If the text file has not loaded yet and DONE does not equal 1, it keeps looping until it has loaded.

When the pre-loader does advance, we get this statement:

```
ifFrameLoaded (1) {
    gotoAndPlay (6);
    /loader:percentage = "10%";
}
```

In addition to the looping animation, we wanted to give the user a percentage loaded indicator. This is simply a dynamic text field on the pre-loader Movie Clip that we gave a variable name of percentage. We simply tell it to display 10% on the pre-loader and go to frame 6 when everything on frame 1 has loaded. On frame 6 it encounters more information to load and a similar script that tells it to advance and show 20% loaded. This continues to happen in 10% increments until 100% has loaded and the pre-loader is done.

When all sections have loaded, the pre-loader tells the opening animation that everything is safe and secure in memory and it is okay to proceed. Instead of abruptly ending the animation and jumping into the site, we told the logo ball to bounce one more time. However, this time the ball fades away as it is going back up and the ripples reverse direction and zoom down into one small point. This is done with a simple series of basic frame actions that tell which section of the animation to play before continuing into the site.

Opening Animation

Amazingly, the entire Design Mentor Flash site is less than 200KB. That's very small for a site that contains so much information. Because the text for the main areas is contained in external text files, that weight is not included.

Even though it's a relatively small site, we still wanted to build an intelligent pre-loader, as I just discussed. We did need to consider what the design of the pre-loader would be. Overall, the site is relatively static, and blue is a dominating color, so we wanted the pre-loader to be both entertaining and not blue.

The Design Mentor logo is in the shape of a basic ball and we came up with the idea of having it bounce up and down during the pre-load from Frank Thomas and Ollie Johnston's book, *The Illusion of Life: Disney Animation*. This is an incredible book every Flash designer should own and read.

It covers the basics of good animation from the masters themselves. In it they talk about the physics of a bouncing ball and how it squishes on impact.

We thought it would be fun to experiment with this using the Design Mentor logo as the ball. Because of the fluid theme we were using on the site, we explored having ripples appear on the surface every time the logo bounced.

Figure 3.21   *Boing-boing.*

To create the ripple, we started with a white circle that we copied but did not yet paste. We then selected the original and proceeded to fade the white away to the background. Under the Modify menu we selected Shape, Soften Fill Edges. This command gives you the ability to apply gradient fades to the edge of shapes. This applies the effect to all edges so our circle was fading both in and out. We then pasted the copy of the original circle in place and offset it a bit so that it would give the illusion of light playing off the ripple, like a solar eclipse. We then selected the original circle and deleted it so the interior of the circle was empty and the exterior faded away like a solar eclipse.

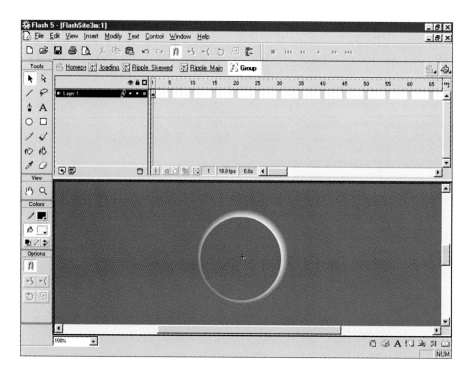

Figure 3.22 *Surf's up.*

We turned this into a Movie Clip and skewed an instance until we liked the shape. We created a new Movie Clip of the skewed ripple and called it Ripple_Skewed. Then we placed multiple copies of Ripple_Skewed on the timeline and tweened them from small and transparent to larger with 100% alpha. We carefully timed the ripple animation to begin when the ball hit the surface. The key to this elegant little animation is the simple offset solar eclipse effect which gives the illusion of the light playing off of the ripples. It creates a sense of depth.

In our loading Movie Clip, we created a looping animation that has the ball bounce up forever. We created this with a simple tween animation of the ball bouncing once. At the end of the bounce we added a gotoAndPlay (1) frame script so it would start over and keep looping. This animation is simple in construction but elegant in design.

Because the opening animation is a complete loop, it would destroy the user's experience if it abruptly stopped and cut to the main site when all the elements are loaded. To avoid this, we used ActionScript to build a somewhat complex pre-loader. This pre-loader is used not only at the beginning of the movie to load all the main elements, but it also is used throughout the site whenever an external text file is called from the main pages. The next section discusses the transition we implemented to the main site.

That's Awfully Revealing

We experimented with many different ways to reveal the main site. We wanted it to snap into place quickly because that's what users expect to see, and we didn't want to hold them from obtaining the information in the site. We also didn't want to just slap them in the face with the site when the pre-loader was finished doing its job.

We played with different means to reveal the site and quickly determined that the least performance-inhibiting method was simply to have two shapes slide offscreen and reveal the main design. Because we are not moving many vector points, and avoiding shape tweens and color effects, we minimize processor impact.

To keep it interesting, we decided to have the ripples reduce to a tiny point—like an old TV turning off—and then slice out to the two shapes that pull away. The effect is nice in that it is primarily gray and reveals the stunning blue drop graphic. The client loved it.

Opening Text Animations

In regard to design, it was important to pull the user in with a simple powerful statement about the client's work. To do this, we pulled out our trusty Swiss Army knife, Swish, and generated the ever-popular text effect. At the time, we hadn't seen it used, but we should have known that it would pop up everywhere soon enough. However, it was and still is effective.

The imagery of the site is elegant, but static, and we wanted the opening text to have some movement and interest. In Swish, we were able to simply type the text in the font we wanted to match the site, apply several effects until we found one we liked, and export it as an SWF. In Flash, we simply imported the SWF and we were in business.

Area Animations

For a few of the main areas of the site, we wanted to add some more interesting animations. For example, as the user comes to the main page of the Client Login screen, the logo morphs into a padlock that closes tight and spins the dial. When the user successfully logs in, the padlock dials a combination and opens. These are simple little animations that add some flavor to the user's experience and don't cost too much bandwidth.

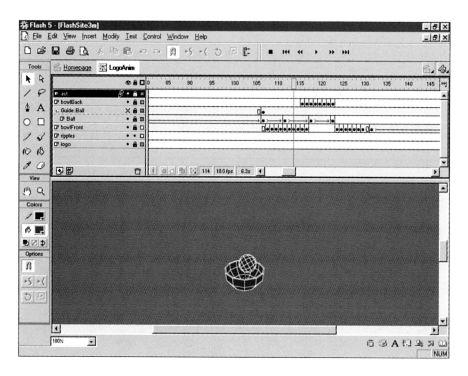

Figure 3.23 *One of the fun animations within the site.*

Design Mentor's CEO is an avid crewer; he was on the M.I.T. crew team and often relates the experience to business. He always says that six men working together as a team can go much faster than six individuals. This was simple enough to build, and because of the business metaphor and the fact that it said something about one of the founders, we felt it was worth integrating into the site.

The funny thing is the first time we made this animation, we had only three rowers and although the client loved the animation, it was quickly pointed out that the boat would perpetually travel in a circle with two rowers on one side and just one on the other. We easily added the fourth rower and we were back on track.

Figure 3.24   *Row, row, row your boat.*

Navigation, Fade Awaaaaaaaaaaaaaaaaaaaay

Because the site would be primarily static, we wanted to add a little life with the buttons. Initially, we experimented with crazy rollovers that had the text enlarge and twist with a neat sound effect. It was quickly apparent that this didn't fit with the company's image. We then played with bright-colored buttons that faded in and out when the user rolled over them. We really liked the design and implemented them all before showing it to the client. This was a mistake, although not a big one.

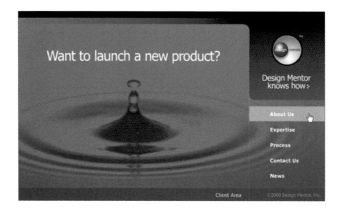

Figure 3.25   *Button effects.*

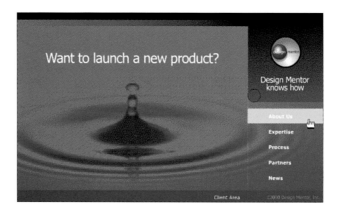

Figure 3.26   *BRITE button effects.*

We were so tied up in the crazy buttons that we felt this latest design was conservative, when in fact it was still too loud. However, everyone liked the fade effect and when we showed it as a subtle gray, the color was quickly approved.

The client did ask to see a different fade rate (how fast the button would disappear when you rolled off). We quickly learned that with a couple dozen buttons, you could spend a lot of time making manual adjustments, so Phil came up with a great idea of building a master fade device that could be easily changed. The solution is quite simple, but might be a bit complex to explain, so I will walk through it carefully.

First, let's look at the Master control. This is the variable that we can change at anytime to control the fade rate of the entire movie. In the first frame of the movie, we have a simple frame script:

```
fadeRatio = "10";
```

This variable will act like the master volume. Whatever value you assign to the `fadeRatio` variable controls the percentage increments the button uses to fade out. The higher the number, the faster the fade. If you set the value to 1, the button fades in one-percent increments, which could take a few seconds. If you set the value to 100 (or 100%), the fade immediately switches from gray to invisible. Open the source file on the CD-ROM and play with the value to see the effect.

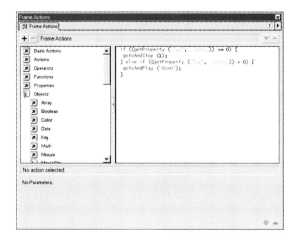

Figure 3.27   *The Fader.*

This device allowed us to accommodate the client's many requests to get the fade just right. Here is how we use this variable.

First, the fade device is built entirely with ActionScripting and is universal. In other words, you could place this device inside any Movie Clip and it would apply the same effect to that Movie Clip as it does to the button. In fact, I guess you could drop it on the main timeline of a movie and it would fade it in and out. No guarantees, but go ahead and try it.

The Fader is a two-layer, three-frame Movie Clip with no elements in it other than a script. Layer one, titled lbls, has a simple frame label in frame two that reads down. When a button is in the down state, it refers to this label.

Frame one of the actions layer, titled act, contains a stop action. This keeps the Fader device inactive until it is called on. The second frame of this layer has the following script:

```
setProperty ("..", _alpha, (getProperty("..", _alpha))-
➡Number(/:fadeRatio));
```

When we tell Fader to go to frame label down, this script then says set the alpha value of ".." (which means the Movie Clip I am in) to a value equal to the Movie Clip's current alpha value minus the value of the fadeRatio variable. Nothing tells the Fader to stop, so it proceeds to the next frame, where it encounters this script:

```
if ((getProperty ( "..", _alpha )) <= 0) {
    gotoAndStop (1);
} else if ((getProperty ( "..", _alpha )) > 0) {
    gotoAndPlay ("down");
}
```

This says that if the property of the Movie Clip that the Fader is located in is less than or equal to zero, go to frame one of Fader and stop. If it isn't less than or equal to zero, it continues on to the 'else if' statement. The else if statement says if the alpha property of the Movie Clip I am in is greater than zero, go to the Fader frame labeled down. This continues and takes away percentage increments of the Movie Clip's alpha value until zero is reached. If the master Fade Ratio is set to 1, this occurs in 1% increments; if it is set to 100%, it happens very quickly. This powerful little device does not care what it is applying this effect to and is therefore very universal.

Now let's talk about how we call this Fader script from the Movie Clip and another well-planned device Phil developed.

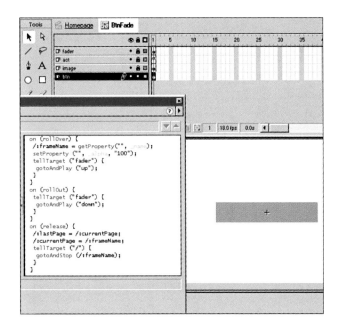

Figure 3.28   *The button.*

The BtnFade Movie Clip was designed to be scalable to fit as any button we need in the movie and still have the same effect as described above. This is accomplished primarily by utilizing a basic rectangle with no outline that can easily be resized with no visible stretching. When the BtnFade Movie Clip is used in the home page movie, an Alpha effect of 0% is applied so that it is not visible until rolled over.

This simple four-layer, single-frame Movie Clip has one layer for the Fader Movie Clip we just covered, one layer for a stop action, one layer for the image you see when you roll over it, and one layer for a button that contains all the action.

The Fader layer and Action layer are self-evident. The Image layer contains an instance of a Movie Clip called box that has been scaled to the correct size and tinted to the color we want displayed when the button is rolled over and the transparency is set to 100%.

On the next layer down, the bottom layer, we have a simple button. This button consists of only a hit area. This keeps it simple and invisible, and we can then control what is seen by the Image element on the layer above this one.

The button element is used solely to handle the actions and has the following script attached:

```
on (rollOver) {
    /:frameName = getProperty("", _name);
    setProperty ("", _alpha, "100");
}
on (rollOut) {
    tellTarget ("fader") {
        gotoAndPlay ("down");
    }
}
on (release) {
    tellTarget ("_root") {
        gotoAndStop (/:frameName);
    }
}
```

Let's look at the rollover state first. On rollover, the script defines a variable called framename by first going to the main timeline and getting the instance name of me. (By *me*, I mean the button the user rolled over.) To keep the code as clean and the solution as intelligent as possible, we have only one Fader Button that we use over and over again. That makes it very important that we first identify which button the user is rolling over so that we apply the fade to the correct one. This is critical!

We intentionally designed each of the main buttons on the main timeline to have EXACTLY the same names as the frame labels of the various areas, case sensitive and all. If we had a section for Job Opportunities marked by a frame label called JobOpportunities, we would give the instance of BtnFade located behind the Job Opportunities text an instance name of JobOpportunities.

Here's why. On rollover, we tell the variable framename to be exactly the name of the button instance we are on. Later, if the user clicks, we simply tell it to go to the frame label called whatever the value of framename is. The critical factor is giving the button instances and the corresponding frame labels exactly the same names.

When the user rolls over an instance of the BtnFade button named AboutUs, the script says make the variable framename contain the value AboutUs. Then the script sets the alpha property of the Movie Clip where the user's mouse is located to 100%, which makes it instantly visible.

In the next section, the script says if the user rolls off the Movie Clip, tell Fader to go to the label down, which begins the incremental process of decreasing the alpha property to zero as described earlier.

If the user does not roll off the button but instead clicks, we tell _root, which is the main timeline of the whole movie, to go to the frame labeled the value of the variable framename (which in this case is AboutUs). It sounds a little complex, but it is actually quite simple if you run through it a couple of times. More importantly, it is very modular and can be used in any movie. Just be careful that you label your buttons and sections the same!

Scroll Bars 101

Because we put the power of content control into the hands of the client, we needed to ensure that the scroll bars were dynamic and appeared only if there is more text than the field can display. There are basically four pieces to the scrollbars: the arrows; the scroll bar drag box; the space between the arrows; and the tracker. Tracker is an empty Movie Clip that only contains an ActionScript that, in a nutshell, coordinates between the dynamic text field and the other scroll bar elements.

Tracker first determines whether the scroll bar should be present, and if so, it ensures that the scroll handle is in the appropriate location compared to the scroll location of the text.

It looks a little complex because there are quite a few lines of ActionScript spread among the various scroll bar elements. After you start identifying each element it should become clear.

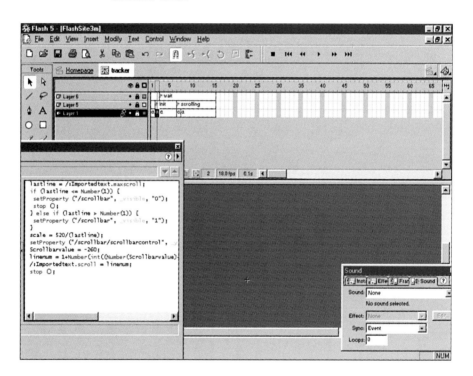

Figure 3.29 *Tracker.*

Let's assume for this discussion that the dynamic text field associated with Importedtext is only 20 lines long. Let's also assume that the text we are inputting into it will be 40 lines long, which means we have 20 lines of text to scroll.

Tracker has four possible states: no scroll bar; initializing; waiting to scroll; and scrolling. The Tracker MC basically has five critical frames with nothing but ActionScripting in each.

Technically, there are more than five frames, but this is simply for organizational purposes so that you can read the frame labels. The extra frames contain no functionality and if we wanted to, we could remove them. This is a simple means to make the files easier to work with.

The first four frames correspond to the four states listed earlier and a final state that loops back to the scrolling state when the user is—you guessed it—scrolling. Let's walk through each of these.

In the default state (state one), Tracker has no scroll bars. This is the first frame of the Tracker movie clip.

```
setProperty ("/scrollbar", _visible, "0");
lastline = Number (0);
linenum = Number (0);
play ();
```

This is the normal state, which assumes that there isn't enough text to make scrolling necessary. It sets the scroll bar Movie Clip with the instance name of `scrollbar` on the main timeline to be invisible. The variable `lastline` defines the number of lines that exceed the display capacity of the dynamic text field. We set this to zero, which means no scrolling is necessary. We will be checking and using this variable in a minute. `linenum` is an important variable that defines which line of the dynamic text should be displayed as the first line of the dynamic text field. If we had a twelve-line paragraph and set `linenum` to 6, you would be scrolled halfway down the text. We will use this in a minute as well.

When the user goes to a page that contains dynamic text, the Tracker is told to initialize, or purge the old variables, and determine whether scrolling is needed on this new page. This is accomplished because the Tracker is constantly looping. In the frame labeled `init`, it analyzes the length of the imported text file where the following code is encountered:

```
lastline = /:Importedtext.maxscroll;
if (lastline < Number(1)) {
    setProperty ("/scrollbar", _visible, "0");
    stop ();
} else if (lastline => Number(1)) {
    setProperty ("/scrollbar", _visible, "1");
}

scale = 520/(lastline);
setProperty ("/scrollbar/scrollbarcontrol", _y, -260);
/:Importedtext.scroll = 1;
stop ();
```

In the first line, `.maxscroll` determines how many lines of text are outside the text field; in this case, we decided it would be 20. Because we have a fixed height window to display the text in, we simply counted the number of lines to be displayed and anything more than that would turn on the scrolling.

The `if` statement determines whether we need to show the scroll bar. If the last line of text is less than one, we assume that no text is appearing below our max line and therefore scrolling does not need to occur, and the scrollbar is set to invisible. If the last line of text is greater than one, scrolling is initialized and the scrollbar is set to visible.

Within this same frame action, we define the variable `scale` to equal 520 divided by the number of lines outside the dynamic text box. 520 is the full range of the scroll bar. When the handle of the scroll bar is in the middle, it is at zero. It can move 260 units, or pixels, in either direction. If we divide 520 by the number of exceeded lines in the display, we come up with a number that serves as a good increment for the handle to move when the user clicks.

The next line of code sets the property of the y variable of the drag box to −260, which is the top of the scroll bar (remember the middle of the scroll bar is zero). Then, the line `/:Importedtext.scroll = 1;` sets which line of text is at the top line of your variable text field (in this case, the first line).

124

Now let's start by looking in the scrollbar Movie Clip and specifically at the arrows. Each arrow just calls to the frame labeled Up or Down in the scrollbar Movie Clip. Down is the same as Up; it just adds values instead of subtracting. Let's just look at Up.

In the ScrollBar Movie Clip frame Up, we encounter the following code:

```
scroller = getProperty("scrollbarcontrol", _y);
newscroll = scroller-(/tracker:scale);
if (Number(newscroll)<Number(-260)) {
    newscroll = "-260";
}
setProperty ("scrollbarcontrol", _y, newscroll);
/tracker:ScrollBarValue = newscroll;
 /tracker:linenum = 1+Number(int((Number(/tracker:
➥Scrollbarvalue)+260) /(/tracker:scale)));
/:Importedtext.scroll = /tracker:linenum;
play ();
```

First, we find out where the scroll bar drag box is with the `getProperty` function. Then we create a variable (`newscroll`) that will show the new position of the drag box by determining the actual position and subtracting the scale from it. Let's say we are at 208. We then subtract the scale, which is 26, and we get 182. The `if` statement is a paranoid check. Just in case something weird happens, we make sure that it cannot go further than the limit at the top or bottom. Then we use the `setProperty` function to set the value of the drag box to the new position, 182, which is the new position we just determined. Then we update the tracker `ScrollBarValue` variable with the value from the `newscroll` variable so it knows where we are. We will then update the variable (`linenum`) that determines what line shows first in the box. Then we tell the movie to move forward with the ever popular Play command.

Next, let's look at the drag box, also called the *drag handle*, and the spaces between it and the up and down arrows.

The drag box needs to be watched as the user drags it so that the text will be updated dynamically as we go.

The drag handle is a button inside an instance of the ScrollBarSlider Movie Clip. We need to control how the text is moved when the user clicks and drags this box, so attached to the ScrollButtonBox button, we have the following:

```
on (press) {
    startDrag ("", false, 0, -260, 0, 260);
tellTarget ("/tracker") {
        gotoAndPlay ("scrolling");
    }
}
```

This basically limits the up and down drag limits and tells the `tracker` Movie Clip to move to the frame labeled `scrolling` where the following code is located to watch us as we drag this up and down:

```
ScrollBarValue = getProperty("/scrollbar/
➡scrollbarcontrol", _y);
linenum = 1+Number(int((Number(Scrollbarvalue)+260)/
➡(scale)));
/:Importedtext.scroll = linenum;
```

The first line gets the drag box's position. We then create a variable from the position of the drag box and the scale. Let's say that, at this split second, the drag box was at 47.678. The preceding calculation takes 47.678 plus 260 divided by the scale (which comes out to 11.833), rounds it to 12, and adds 1, which equals 13. We add 1 because otherwise the very last line would not show. We are not sure why this happens in Flash, but our solution works and that is the primary motivator when you have looming deadlines. So, it then sets the top line of text to the 13th line. That means the user, with some help from our scripting, has just successfully dragged the scroll handle to move the text to the 13th line. Simple, right?

Now, back in the ScrollBarControl on the drag box button is
the script:

```
on (release) {
    tellTarget ("/tracker") {
        gotoAndStop ("wait");
    }
    stopDrag ();
    /tracker:ScrollBarValue = getProperty("", _y);
}
```

The on release command just tells the Tracker to stop
tracking our movements. You don't have to use the
`stopDrag()` command, but it would be the same as dipping
your hand in a bucket of superglue and answering the
phone. You better like that phone because it is now a
permanent part of you. The last line updates the Tracker
with our current position.

The last thing is the spaces between the arrows and the
drag box. The user should be able to click in these areas
and scroll down. These guys do basically the same thing as
the arrows do. They just need to update their own position.
On the bottom layer of ScrollBarSlider are two invisible
buttons (one for up and one for down) that control this.
Let's look at the button in the lower space, where we find
this script:

```
on (press, keyPress "<Down>") {
    ..:scrollerdn = getProperty("", _y);
    ..:newscrolldn = Number(..:scrollerdn)
      ➥+Number(/tracker:scale);
    if (Number(..:newscrolldn)>260) {
        ..:newscrolldn = "260";
    }
    setProperty ("", _y, ..:newscrolldn);
    /tracker:ScrollBarValue = getProperty("", _y);
    /tracker:linenum = 1+Number(int((Number(/tracker:
      ➥Scrollbarvalue)+260) / (/tracker:scale))));
    /:Importedtext.scroll = /tracker:linenum;
}
```

This is really straightforward if you walk through it line by line. When the user presses down, we determine where the current scroll location is and move accordingly. There is a check in place to make sure that the scroll cannot exceed 260 if going down or −260 if going up. We then give Tracker an update to our new location, tell Tracker where the new text location will be, and the last line of text actually tells the text to move.

Whew! That's it. If you walk through it a couple of times with the source file open, you will see that it is not that difficult to understand.

The Third Dimension

The granddaddy animation of the site is the one we built for logo definition. What do I mean? The Design Mentor logo has some meaning to its shape. You can see this in the About Us section of the site. The purpose of this animation is to hint at the meaning behind the Design Mentor logo, which is really just a ball in a bowl. A ball in a bowl, you say? The concept is that the ball rolling around in the bowl mimics the process Design Mentor goes through on every project. Constantly working in full circle between planning, implementing, testing, and back to planning while constantly documenting.

This clearly would not come across by viewing the logo alone, but we felt there was never a reason actually to explain this to the viewer. We felt it would be neat to show the logo in 3D and also to explain the process, but to let the user make the connection. This is far more interesting than explaining everything.

3D in Flash is very exciting, very neat, and also very much an illusion. I say this because there is no plug-in or 3D element to Flash. When people talk about 3D in Flash, they are really talking about digitizing a series of 3D images into the vector format that Flash can import and display. The latest craze about 3D in Flash really has to do with the newly available tools that streamline the process of converting a variety of 3D formats such as 3DS and DXF into an SWF file.

I understand that as I am writing this, more and more 3D tools are becoming available, but the one that is currently dominating the market is Swift 3D. First, let's step back even farther than that and talk about some of the tools we used to create these 3D elements before we brought them into Swift 3D for conversion into vectors. With the growing popularity of 3D and the desire to create unique elements, you will soon find a situation in which you will want to incorporate 3D into your Flash creations.

There are, and have been for many years now, a number of beginner to professional 3D modeling tools. I don't want to cover them all; instead, I will talk about two that I use on a regular basis. The first is a product that used to be available only on the Mac, but is now available on the PC: formZ.

formZ is a powerful full-feature modeling package with a very CAD-like interface. It has a relatively steep learning curve and is not cheap; it costs more than $1,000. It is not a beginner's package and it is not for the faint of heart. It takes dedication and a lot of manual reading before you can use it efficiently. Having said that, formZ offers a great deal of power and a number of professional-level tools to begin creating 3D elements.

I typically use formZ when I know I will be spending a relatively significant amount of time modeling or if I need to build a complex shape. If I am just building a basic shape or an element that does not have to be perfect, I prefer to use Strata Studio Pro.

Strata Studio Pro, now called Strata 3D Pro, is a basic 3D modeling package with some advanced features such as Boolean modeling and raytrace rendering. Don't know what this means? Let me quickly give you the skinny. *Boolean modeling* is the process of creating one shape by adding or subtracting multiple shapes. *Raytracing* is a line-level rendering process that allows for detailed renderings with

129

light effects and shadows. These are features that you typically do not find on entry-level 3D programs.

In Strata, it is easy to create line shapes in FreeHand or Illustrator, bring them in as EPS's, and then manipulate them into the 3D shape you want. This is how we created the 3D bowl for the Design Mentor logo. The best part about Strata is that it is offering a free version of Strata 3D on its Web site. If you like it and want more powerful features, you spend the money and upgrade to Strata 3D Pro for a few hundred bucks.

We started with the basic cross section of the bowl and imported it into Strata. We then carefully lined up the shape and lathed it into the bowl. Lathing creates multiple instances of the line shape and turns it into a 3D shape. Our 3D bowl is just one simple line that is repeated every 10 degrees 36 times. 10 times 36 equals 360 degrees. Voila, a bowl!

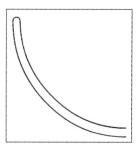

Figure 3.30   *Lathing the bowl with this basic shape.*

Swift 3D imports only the 3ds format and, of course, the older version of Strata I have does not allow you to export in 3ds format. I don't believe newer versions do either. So, I hit the Web and found a great little utility called Crossroads by Keith Rule. This utility allows you to open DXF files, which Strata can export to, and a variety of other 3D formats and export them to 3ds. I was very disappointed to learn this about Swift 3D and very excited to have found Crossroads.

Every 3D program is different, but each one should allow you to control the polygon count of the models you produce and export. This is very important because it has a direct impact on the final file size of the finished SWF file. The polygon count of a 3D model is basically the number of polygons required to build the shape. The fewer polygons used, the smaller the file size.

In the case of the bowl described earlier, instead of lathing it every 10 degrees and having 36 segments, we could have lathed it every 20 degrees and had only 18 segments, which would have had fewer polygons and eventually a smaller SWF file. Let me illustrate in extremes. We could have lathed the bowl with four segments; it would be a very small file size, but it would look awfully rough. You see this in a lot of video games in which the shapes are intended to be round, but if you look closely they are a series of angles. This is so that the polygonal count is lower and the action on the screen can be rendered faster.

We could also go to the other end of the spectrum and lathe the bowl 720 times or every half a degree. The level of detail would be excellent and it would appear very smooth. However, the file size would be huge!

We experimented several times until we found a good balance. Because the 3D bowl would be on screen for only a few seconds and moving, we could afford a lower polygon count. Another factor that has a major impact on file size is the rendering format you output the animation to.

Swift 3D offers a variety of rendering formats but they really boil down to three: an outline of the shape, each polygon with a basic flat fill, or each polygon with a gradient fill to simulate smoothness.

There is a huge difference in final file size depending on the output choice. I recommend that you plan to spend a significant amount of time experimenting with your project before you decide. We were lucky with this project. Because the client was a group of product engineers, it made sense to show the shapes in wire frame, or outline, format. This lent to the overall feel nicely and saved a great deal of file size. If you need to have smooth animations and smooth shapes, plan to have a huge file.

Finally, you need to plan the frame rate at which you will export the animations. It is tempting to go very high, but think it through first. Most animations of more than 18 frames a second are wasting bandwidth. 18 frames per second is a lot of information. Most computers will be okay, but some will struggle to keep up with frame rate. Additional frames per second will add little value, but a lot of bandwidth, and slow many machines to a crawl. Play around with different variables and see what kind of impact they have.

After the files are in Flash, take the time to break apart each symbol. You will often get multiple lines on top of each other that add nothing visually, but slow down the redraw and increase the file size. Some lines will not line up properly either. It is a bit painstaking, but well worth the effort.

We now had the 3D logo digitized and ready for animation. Our plan was to take the standard 2D logo, morph it into the 3D bowl, and have the ball circle around in it. This meant we needed to get a digital copy of the 2D logo. The only electronic files the client had were raster versions of the logo. We knew that making the transition from a bitmap of the logo to a vector version would not look great.

So, we jumped in to Macromedia FreeHand and quickly redrew the logo and exported to a SWF that easily, and cleanly, imported into Flash. In FreeHand, we focused on drawing the basic shapes and applied the gradient fills in Flash. FreeHand 9.0 gradients do not translate as cleanly into Flash as staring from scratch in Flash. Now that we had a 2D, vector version of the logo, we could easily continue with our logo animation work and finish the project.

Version Detection

As development on the Flash site began to wind down and testing started, we shifted our focus to the users' experience as they first come to the site. We knew that users would arrive at DesignMentor.com with a variety of browsers and different versions of the Flash plug-in. Early on, we determined that the site had to be built in Flash 4 because we assumed that most of the users would have this plug-in. It was tempting to use the features of Flash 5; we will cover some of them in the Hookumu.com case study.

This meant that all we really had to be concerned about was users who didn't have the plug-in at all and users with Flash 3 plug-in or earlier. We never wanted the browser to show the puzzle piece icon indicating that the user could not see the site. We felt that this would reflect on the reputation, or brand, of Design Mentor.

What we came up with to ensure that this would not happen is a variety of Flash and JavaScript tricks. First, we created a very well-designed, but fast-loading index page.

This page gives the users the option of viewing a clean and simple HTML site or viewing the Flash site. This is important and I want to talk about this for a moment. Many sites do not offer this choice, but I think you should propose it to the user. If a person is coming to a site to just receive some basic information, such as contact info, she should not be forced to load a plug-in, and then load the site, and then hunt down the info. It defeats the purpose. It is a bit of extra work to develop the site in HTML, but doing so will serve the users well.

In the case of DesignMentor.com, we had very little content, so we decided to keep the HTML site as simple and fast loading as possible. I would like to talk about something that frustrates me every time I see it. Have you ever been surfing the Web and you come to a homepage where they give you the choice of a fast site or a slow site? The fast site is typically an HTML site and the slow site is typically a

Flash site. This is crazy! If you add up all the code and images in the slow site, it probably weighs three times what the Flash site weighs.

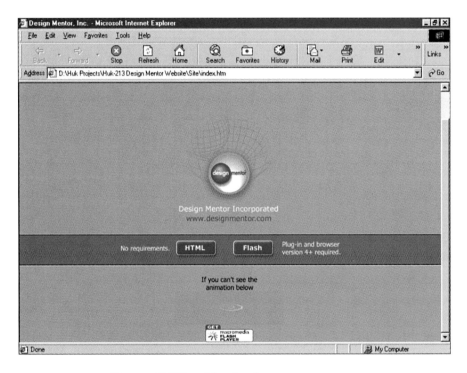

Figure 3.31 *Plug-in please.*

Designers and developers are giving Flash a bad name by developing Flash-only sites that are very heavy and slow loading. This is like buying a Ferrari and using it to tow a boat!

Flash is tremendous at delivering a great deal of information in a very small file size. Everyone seems to be creating these rich-media Web sites in Flash, which are just Web sites with huge and horrible audio and slow boring animations. We will talk about how to create Flash Web sites with audio and many animations in the Hookumu.com case study; there we will show you how to do it without making the user wait at all. If you want to do this, go for it, but give the user a small, fast-loading Flash choice as well.

For Design Mentor, our purpose for the HTML site was to serve those users who did not have the plug-in, and did not want to go get it.

We indicate on the main page that the user will need the Flash plug-in to see the site. But we also built a small Flash file that detects whether users have the plug-in. If they do not have it, the site displays a GIF indicating that no plug-in was detected. This is done with some simple HTML and JavaScript that you can see on the site for yourself.

If they do have the plug-in, we need to ensure that it is at least version 4. This is often overlooked, and users with the version 3 plug-in can become frustrated not knowing why they can't correctly see the site. This is a bigger issue with Flash 5 solutions; when users have version 4.0, it will appear to work but produce very weird results.

This code will detect the version. I do not recall exactly who the author of this code is, but thank you to Flashkit.com for making it available on its site and the original author. If anyone knows the author, please let me know so I can make the appropriate credits on the Hookumu site.

```
// This script parses the $version variable to
// find out what platform, major and minor versions
// of the Flash Player the user has. This script will
// reveal whether the user is on Mac, Windows, or Unix,
// as well as any other platforms the player may be
// released for in the future.
//
// For best results, use this script in a movie, export
// as a version 4 SWF, and use it in your detection
➥routine.
//
playerVersion = eval("$version");
myLength = length(playerVersion);
while (i<=myLength) {
        i = i+1;
        temp = substring(playerVersion, i, 1);
        if (temp eq " ") {
                platform = substring(playerVersion, 1,
                ➥i-1);
```

```
                        majorVersion = substring(playerVersion,
                        ➥i+1, 1);
                        secondHalf = substring(playerVersion,
                        ➥i+1, myLength-i);
                        minorVersion = substring(secondHalf, 5,
                        ➥2);
                }
        }
        //
        // The $version variable was not present in the earliest
        // releases of the Flash Player 4. This part will catch
        ➥that.
        //
        if (majorVersion>=4) {
                // They have a Flash Player 4 or later, release
                ➥11 or later
        } else {
                // They have a Flash Player 4, release 10 or
                ➥earlier
                majorVersion = "4";
        }
        //
        // You can decide to send the user to a different page,
        // based on whether they have a Flash Player 4 or 5
        //
        if (majorVersion eq "4") {
                nextScene ();
        } else if (majorVersion eq "5") {
                nextScene ();
                // Send the user to a Flash 5 page
        }
        //
        // You can also check the minor version to see if the
        // user's player supports features like web printing.
        //
        if (minorVersion>20) {
        // They have a player capable of native web printing.
        }
```

The preceding code is very simple and you don't need to
understand it for it to function—just copy and paste it into
a new, first scene of your Flash file. In this scene, place text
that says wrong, or older, plug-in detected. If the users

have v3.0 or earlier, the text is displayed and the user can click on the Get Flash button we have included.

If the users do have the correct plug-in, it plays the next scene in which we display a constant looping animation of some water ripples.

Another cool little trick we implemented was the new window effect. Using JavaScript, we launch a new window with no controls and no scrolling, and we display the Flash site there. As that is loading, we tell the main window to display a new HTML page where we thank the users for visiting and offer a link back to the main HTML page.

This is cool because when the users close the Flash window, they are not staring at the same site they thought they just left. Instead, we thank them and let them go back if necessary. The key is that the second page must be very small in overall page weight because it will be fighting for bandwidth as the Flash site is loading. It is a neat little trick that has been well received by Design Mentors users.

Post-Mortem

Overall, the project has been a great success. The balance of a clean professional design with a leading-edge technology communicates the message Design Mentor was looking to communicate with its Web site. I believe a major reason for the site's success was our constant awareness of the message and the users' experience. We avoided large animations and complex, difficult-to-use interfaces.

As always, there are a few things we would like to change and are doing so in subsequent maintenance projects to the site. This is normal and expected; as clients become familiar with their sites, they can always find exciting new things to do with it. Our scalable architecture and design can easily accommodate these requests.

One area of the site that we are changing significantly is the secure component we called the Client Area. For the first version of the site, the clients knew they wanted the ability to post project documents in a secure location, but they did not have all the details worked out, nor did they want to delay the launch date. We decided to implement a simple form that would check for a default username and password and return either an error or a sample area for Design Mentor to showcase to their clients. We did this knowing that a more robust solution would be built shortly after the launch. In another case study, I will discuss how Hookumu.com utilized this system to work with confidential data.

Although the scroll bars we built function quite well, they do not have the performance or scalability we wanted. Had this been a Flash 5 solution, we would have used the scroll bars I talk about in the Hookumu.com Web site. However, the scroll bars meet the client's needs, and shortly thereafter, we were able to develop Flash 5 scroll bars for Hookumu.com, which I will cover in the next chapter.

Another element we would like to change is to make the dynamic text area of the site able to display basic HTML. Phil assures me that this is possible and we are working on it now for another project. HTML capabilities will allow both us and the client to have greater control over how the information is displayed.

There has been some discussion about creating a scalable version of the site that fills the screen regardless of the user's display size. Although these solutions can be attractive, they have their limitations and need special consideration when developing them. It is difficult to work with bitmap backgrounds, such as the water drop, because quality begins to degrade as you scale JPEGs. In general, if you intend to design a solution that takes over the user's entire screen, consider that this might be intrusive—particularly when the user has intentionally positioned and sized his Web browser. If this is not an issue for your solution, just ensure that navigational controls are obvious and recognizable at both very small and very large screen sizes.

Finally, concerning the design, there is little I would change with the exception of refining some of the animations. DesignMentor.com is currently nominated for several design awards and we hope it will take some home. Either way, it is a project we are proud of but, more importantly, it is a successful solution for our client.

CHAPTER **4**

Hookumu.com

Another Flash site—Flash 5 this time.

Overview

"Another Flash-based Web site," you ask? "Didn't you cover this already? What more could I possibly need to know?" Enough to dedicate a chapter to it, I think.

Initially, I chose another project to write about for this chapter, but as we were developing Hookumu.com, I decided there could be a lot to learn here. After we finished DesignMentor.com, we had a fresh perspective on how to improve upon the process of building a Flash-only Web site. That isn't to say we thought we could improve on DesignMentor.com (especially if they're reading this book), but because hindsight is 20/20.

We also decided that Hookumu.com needed to be built in Flash 5. We wanted to take advantage of the new features and we felt our potential clients would be comfortable downloading the latest plug-in to see what we were capable of.

In this chapter, you'll learn how to use some of the new ActionScripting commands and syntax as well as how to load external movies. I would also like to give you a deeper glimpse into the design process and show you some of the preliminary designs we considered before settling on the solution you now see. I will also show you how we used some of the free ActionScripting code available on the Web to take advantage of advanced features without spending a great deal of time mastering scripting.

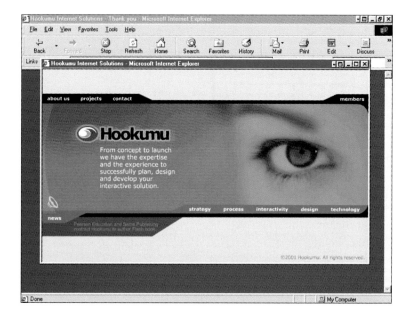

Figure 4.1 *The final solution.*

The Players

Think about some of the tougher clients you have had—how critical they were of your solutions and how they nitpicked. Then think about how you struggled to get the design or functionality just right. How you refined it and achieved near-perfection and stood proudly next to it as you presented it to the clients, only to have them tear it apart. It can be very frustrating. Now take those clients and make them ten, twenty, or a hundred times worse. That is what our client was like. Our client was us.

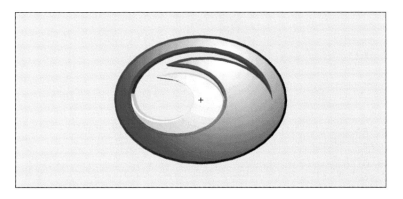

Figure 4.2   *The Hookumu logo.*

Creating solutions for yourself, or your own company, can be a challenging prospect. It's easy to let deadlines slip as you continue to try and reach perfection. Because you are your own client, compromising deadlines can be tempting. After all, you're not going to yell at yourself, are you?

As tough as all this is, it's worse when the project you're creating will be an example to the entire world, your clients and competition included, of what your capabilities are. When what you are building is what you will be presenting as your best work, you are never satisfied.

We struggled with this. Our saving grace was the knowledge that a number of large projects were on the horizon and we knew we had to finish the site now or deal with bigger problems in the future.

At this point, Hookumu was still just me doing most of the work. Several people assisted at different times during a project, including Phil Stephenson who takes care of the more advanced ActionScripting. We had three contractors, two of whom were pure technology and database developers and one who helped with design and production. Hookumu was starting to become a very solid team.

The Client's Need: Introducing Hookumu.com

At this point, Hookumu was just a few months and a few projects old, but it was clear we were going to be successful. Our client list was growing even though we didn't have a live Web site yet.

Figure 4.3   *The first Hookumu.com placeholder page.*

We had registered the domain, and set up e-mail, FTP, and a simple placeholder page. This was enough to let us think we would never have to endure the experience of building a site for ourselves. I'm making this sound worse than it is. We were very excited about finding the time to build the site correctly, but we understood that we would be the most demanding client we had ever had and, at the same time, that we were willing to compromise milestones and deliverables like we never would for a client. It was the worst client you could imagine teaming up with a development team willing to let the project slide. Yikes!

Our client list was growing solely from referrals. Having clients recommend your services is the best business development tool. To get a client to recommend you, you simply need to deliver what you promised and exceed expectations. That's not always so easy, but if you do the proper planning, every project can be a success. The client referrals were going a long way and most clients didn't ask too many questions about the company. But as our clients were changing from local businesses to national corporations, they began to inquire more.

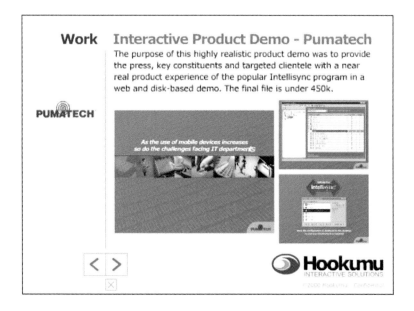

Figure 4.4 *We didn't have a site yet, so we would post this demo for prospective clients.*

Suddenly our own Web site was doing us harm. The biggest issue we had was convincing new clients that we could handle projects larger in scope than our examples. We had experience from our other jobs, but our site made us look like newbies to the industry and a client referral can only go so far to address this concern.

Suddenly, we were violating one of our own cardinal rules. For years, I had been telling clients to stay away from Internet development firms that had bad sites. If a firm couldn't build a good site for itself, how could it build one for the client? This was easy to enforce when we had built sites for our past employers that could stand this test—particularly when all the development firms were so busy that they built junk Web sites for themselves. Now we were on the other side of the table.

We decided it could not be put off any longer. We needed a site that would communicate to prospective clients what our core services were, what our capabilities were, and in general, some messages about our philosophies and process. And, of course, we needed a way to showcase our past projects and client referrals.

The Solution

Now that we had decided to move forward with site development, we had to put up a quick solution that would meet the needs of general inquiries while we were developing the final solution. In Flash, we quickly built a glorified slideshow presentation that spoke about our services, strengths, and unique approach, and showcased three of our latest projects including references from these same clients.

The piece was built small enough to e-mail to any general inquiries we had, and also so it could be shown on our Web site and at initial client meetings. This held the lions at bay for a while, but we knew the big clients (and the competition) would not let us get away with it. We were in discussion with Houghton Mifflin, Bose Corporation, and the LEGO Group, and those companies only work with firms offering exceptional and established services. Our site needed to reflect our capabilities in the same light.

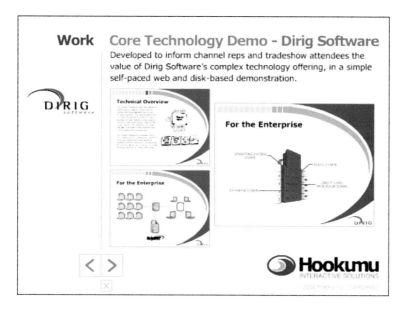

Figure 4.5   *Our demo/site/presentation says, "Hey, we are better than what our site shows! We just can't find time to build it!"*

Information Architecture

As with any site we develop, we first started with an information architecture. In this case, the first approach ended up being quite a bit different than the final results.

For our first information architecture, we took into account everything we wanted Hookumu.com to be. This included products currently on the drawing board that won't be to market until 2002, as well as an Investors section and a job posting area. However, Hookumu wasn't ready for all this. Our game plan was to spend the next three quarters building a client base and a technical team to complement our design group. Only then would we need to start developing products and searching for seed funding.

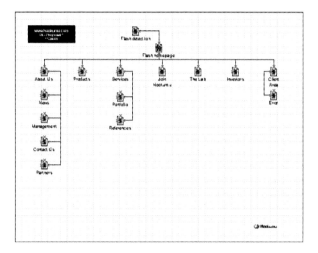

Figure 4.6 *Initial information architecture for Hookumu.com.*

It was clear we needed to slim down the information architecture to better represent where our business currently was. We determined that we wanted to the site to be as focused and straightforward as possible. We would keep the typical About Us section, which would include a way to contact Hookumu, but felt that a section about our management team was unnecessary because it was really just me doing all the management! First, we had to line up the key talent and team leaders, and then we had to showcase them on the site—not the other way around.

Along the same lines as the management section, it was clear we didn't need an investors (or partners) section yet. Only after we had the exact business plans, product prototypes, and a clear path of funding needs would we begin to attract investors and have a section on the site to service them. So, needless to say, this section was axed from the final version of the information architecture.

We wanted to keep the area for dynamic news. However, as exciting as the news in this section is to us, we believed that most clients would be more interested in our overall offerings. They could gather the rest of the information through interviews. So, we decided to simply to display one of the many headlines from our news section in the lower-left corner.

We wanted to talk about our services and also showcase some of the projects we worked on. We were sooooooo bored with the way most companies in the business do this with an Our Services section and a Gallery section. Aside from that boredom, we also didn't want a Gallery section because this tends to label you as a design-only firm. Although we feel our designs are exceptional, we offer expertise in technical services as well. We used the Projects section to kill two birds with one stone. We felt that the label was appropriate and by letting the examples speak for themselves it would also describe what our capabilities are.

We still needed to clarify just what Hookumu did, so we decided a set of inconspicuous sub-navigation buttons that identified our services would be the best approach. Determining exactly what we would list proved to be the greatest challenge. At one end of the spectrum, we could list every technical and design program and language we knew; at the other end, we could just say we were Internet specialists. Neither seemed appropriate.

We took a white board and listed every service we provided to our customers: design, consulting, strategy, development, production, Flash, Microsoft, XML, HTML, DHTML, SQL dB development, and on and on. The list could easily fill two pages. We then started identifying groups that each of these services fell into and came up with the following three: strategy, design, and technology.

That was good, but a couple of key components were missing that are critical differentiators for Hookumu. One is the process and approach we take to every project. This is not necessarily a service but a discrete component of all our projects that makes Hookumu successful. We decided the best term for this page would be *Process*.

Another key component not properly represented in the overly simplified IA was interactivity. Design and Technology covers what we do in Flash, but it doesn't come close to covering the end product. We needed a way to illustrate that combining design and technology with a purpose creates a finished product greater than the sum of its parts. You've heard that before. So, we called this last area *Interactivity* and had our final list.

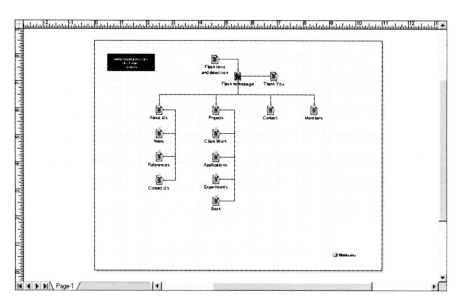

Figure 4.7 *The final information architecture. Never say final!*

Design Evolution

Within each section, we wanted a unique animation and a paragraph about the particular service. Something visual that reinforced the message. It was tempting to make each area animation entirely unique with a completely independent animation. We decided against this for two particular reasons: time and bandwidth.

We were overdue in launching a site and client projects were piling up. We needed a site soon, and unique, well-designed animations take time. We felt that the most expensive thing we had was time, and the return on investment of spending this time on lengthy animations just wasn't worth it.

We also took into consideration the amount of bandwidth
that these animations would take up. Together, these were
two strong arguments against having several individual
animations. Instead, we decided to get more bang out of
our main illustration: the eye.

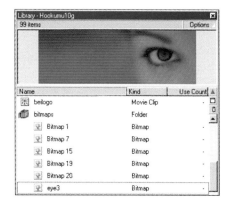

Figure 4.8   *Eye see you.*

The eye is a critical component of our homepage design. It
evolved through many design iterations. We wanted an
image that grabbed the viewer and yet was generic enough
that it could hold up against a variety of content that would
potentially appear next to it. The image had to engage the
viewer; that is, it had to have a bit of mystery, and hold
several potential meanings for the viewer. This was a
difficult task. The eye gave us compelling imagery without
getting specific. It would have been impossible for us to
find an image that was specific to every potential client's
need. Therefore, we needed to be a bit abstract and felt
that the eye accomplished our goal.

From the very first design that included the eye, we were
sold on the idea. The first few designs we could have sold
to Revo—we designed a pair of sunglasses on top of an
orange eye. It looked very cool but it was also very
inappropriate. We knew the eye was going to stay, but we
needed to let it stand on its own and focus on the design
of the elements around it. Take a look at the design
evolution shots in Figure 4.9 to see what I'm talking about.

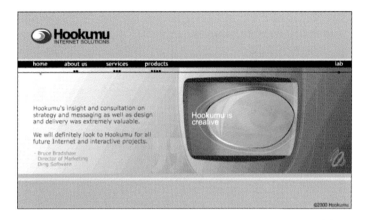

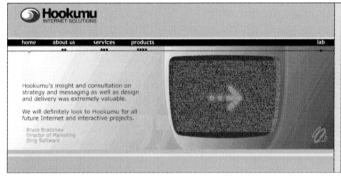

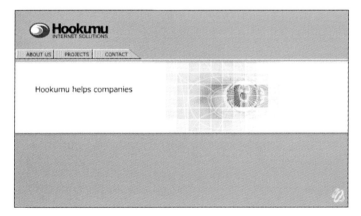

Figure 4.9 *The Hookumu.com design evolution.*
(Continues)

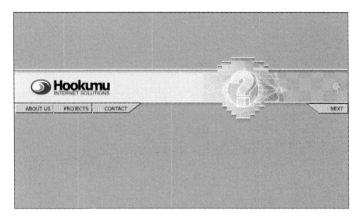

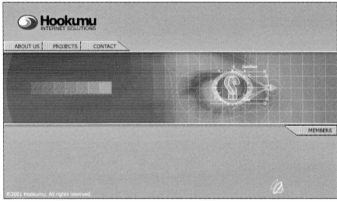

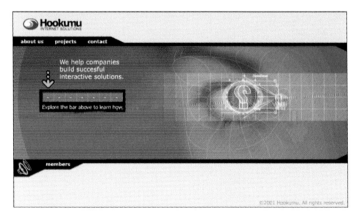

Figure 4.9 *The Hookumu.com design evolution.*
(Continued)

We acquired the eye from Photodisc.com, an online royalty-free stock photography resource. Photodisc is an excellent resource for designers, but be careful: What you use in your design will eventually be a part of someone else's design. That's the nature of stock photography. As in the case of the Hookumu site, when we use stock photography we try to manipulate it substantially to make it unique to our design. For the eye, we actually performed a lot of cropping, colorizing, and blurring to get the perfect design we were looking for. It was now time to conceptualize each individual section design.

Figure 4.10   *Note the data bits over the eye.*

Because we were developing in Flash, we needed to capture the feel of a living, thinking, interactive solution. It was tempting to have elements moving all over the screen with cool sound effects and rollovers, but we also had to ensure that it wasn't distracting, confusing, and gimmicky. What we settled on was a series of simple data bits that randomly scroll across the eye and a cursor that occasionally slides over to the eye, clicks, and fades away. Not only did this add the feel we were looking for, but it also provided us with a common device and theme for the additional eye animations.

We had a distinctive animation for each of the five sections: strategy, process, interactivity, design, and technology. In each, we introduced a unique design element on top of the eye and placed content to the left of it. You should view the site and look at each design; they are interesting, and we get a good deal of positive feedback on these designs.

Figure 4.11   *Each section of the site has a unique animation over the eye. (Continues)*

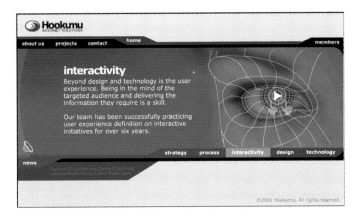

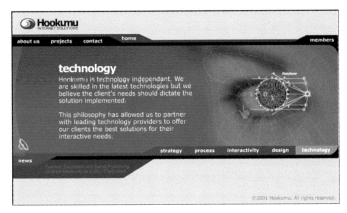

Figure 4.11 *Each section of the site has a unique animation over the eye. (Continued)*

With all the core animations and the information architecture in place, it was now time to focus on the navigation. On any given screen, there could be a number of devices just a click away from the user. We needed to ensure that this was intuitive to the users without giving them too many complex choices. We decided on a navigation scheme that would be consistent throughout the site: Every button would have a normal, rollover, and active state. This seems like a no-brainer, but it's still something you need to consider. We also wanted to ensure that the user could quickly identify what a button was.

Figure 4.12   *Lots of buttons to consider.*

I'm a strong believer in giving the user an interaction model to follow. Typically, the users don't understand what this is, and you don't really want them to understand it. To me, an interaction model is a consistent navigation scheme that allows users to understand what a button is without having to think about it. For example, if you take a look at Yahoo!, you'll see that its simple interaction model is to represent every link by underline text.

For Hookumu.com, our links would be angular buttons with text in them that highlighted when you rolled over them. As with any design, there were some basic exceptions to the rules (for instance the scroll bar buttons) but we felt our plan was safe and consistent. It's important that you give your projects this same level of consideration. In the end, it is these details that make sites easy or difficult to navigate.

Choosing Flash 5

We were still focusing mostly on design when Flash construction began. We had been using Flash 5 for a while, but most of our exports were for the Flash 4 player. No matter how many times I read statistics, analysis reports, and technology sites that indicate what version browsers and plug-ins most users have, I rarely trust the information and typically play it safe.

I know this is no fun, but remember we are talking about real-world case studies here. Whether the solution is for Furniture.com clients or kids playing with LEGO bricks, it's safer to assume that they are not an early adopter of technology than it is to develop a solution for the client that most of its users can't use or won't download the latest plug-in to use.

However, in this case, we were the client and we don't really care what we think of ourselves. It was during Flash development that we ran into Flash 4 limitations that caused us to dive into releasing the site in Flash 5.

The most obvious scripting limitation was with detecting what portion of the site is loaded into memory before playing the movie. The `IfFramesLoaded` syntax was being depreciated and was to be replaced by `_FramesLoaded`. Both are Flash 4–compatible, but we had script libraries that were tested and true using `IfFramesLoaded` and until that point, we did not want to slow down to test `_FramesLoaded`. We realized we had to become proficient and we also wanted to measure the number of frames loaded in external movies. It was clearly time to step up to the latest syntax.

For the preloader, I wanted a continuous looping device that indicated to the viewers that the site was working and not frozen. I also wanted to indicate to the users how much of the site had loaded so that they could anticipate how much longer they needed to wait. Initially, we were going to do this with a percentage bar like we did with DesignMentor.com, but for some reason it didn't fit the design. Instead, we opted to have a status bar that would progress across the screen from left to right. When the bar reached the right side, the site would be fully loaded and the entire status bar would glow white, disappear, and then the black frame would separate to reveal the homepage.

To accomplish the progressing status bar, we built ten of the following scripts. Each instance of the script is responsible for loading approximately ten percent of the site. As ten percent of the site loaded, the status bar increased one step and the next ten percent proceeded to load. I won't cover every step; I've talked enough about preloaders in this book. However, I do want to talk about how to do it with the new syntax.

```
if (_framesloaded>=_totalframes) {

  gotoAndPlay ("preloader", "InterfaceAnim");
} else if ((_framesloaded/_totalframes)*100>=85) {
  play ();
} else {
  gotoAndPlay (34);
}
```

In this example, we first do a global check to see whether the number of frames loaded into memory is greater than or equal to the total number of frames. If the number of frames loaded into memory equals the total frames in the movie, it means the entire site is loaded and can begin playing. If the total number of frames loaded is less than the total frames in the movie, the entire movie has not loaded and it continues to loop until this is true. We do this at about every 10% and update the status bar every time another 10% has loaded.

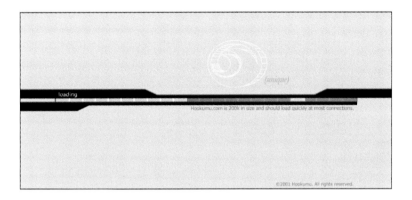

Figure 4.13   *That's a purty preloader, mister.*

We determine the percent of the movie loaded by dividing the number of frames loaded by the total frames (which will result in a decimal) and multiplying this by 100 in order to compare to 100% of the movie loaded. Simple math, but still it doesn't make it necessary to use Flash 5; Flash 4 can handle this just fine. We used Flash 5 for two reasons: to become familiar with the new syntax, and to check the percentage of frames loaded in an external movie. In the preloader, we weren't checking external movies, but we needed to do this later when loading experiments and client work. This wasn't possible in Flash 4 and it was something we wanted to explore in Flash 5.

To keep overall downloads to a minimum, we architected the site to load specific components and content only when necessary. Nothing new here, but we did want to correctly determine when the movie had completely loaded before playing it, particularly in the case of audio.

Audio

As bandwidth increases and easy-to-use audio generation programs become available, custom-generated music and scores are regular client requests. At Hookumu, we are by no means composers or songwriters, but we do possess a professional level of audio capabilities that we offer to our clients and we wanted to showcase this on the site in a passive manner. In other words, we didn't want to call out that we do audio generation, but in case of an inquiry, we could point to the site.

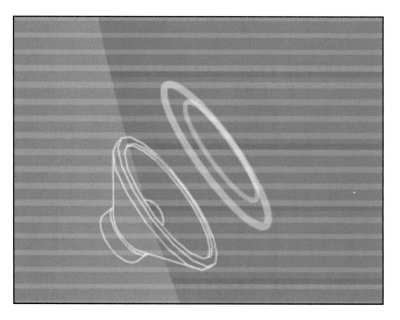

Figure 4.14   *Play that funky music.*

We spent a little time in our audio programs such as ACID and GrooveMaker, mastering an appropriate song with techno undertones and riffs. We then brought it into ACID where we segmented the piece and ensured that it looped seamlessly. It was now Flash-ready.

To add to the whole audio experience, we created a small 3D looping speaker animation. This piece was simple and fun to build. We lathed a simple shape in Strata to resemble a speaker and added small circle animations to represent the sound waves.

We have strong opinions about not making users wait for music unless they choose to do so. Nothing is more disappointing to me than waiting several minutes while the "loading" message loops over and over, only to learn that I waited all that time for an audio score when all I really wanted was the information on the page.

We decided we would load the audio only if the user chose to do so. This meant having a button that would display the loading message until the external audio file was loaded. Until Flash 5, this was not easily accomplished.

The 3D speaker had an invisible button over it that, when pressed, told the speaker to begin loading the external audio file with the following script:

```
/:music = "true";
loadMovie ("audio.swf", "/speaker/audioloaded");
audioBytesTotal = audioloaded.getBytesTotal();
play ();
```

The first line tells the `music` variable on the main timeline to be set to true. This variable is defined so we can check it at any point in the movie to determine whether the audio is playing. I should mention that at this point, Flash 5 had just been released and we weren't always consistent throughout our scripting with the latest syntax. Sometimes you will see a blending of Flash 4 and Flash 5 syntax. This is okay and is supported by Flash and the players, but it is a good practice to stay focused on the latest syntax. Doing so will help you stay current on features as Macromedia releases new product versions.

The second line of script tells the external movie `audio.swf` to be loaded into a Movie Clip on the stage with an instance name of `audioloaded`. By loading it into another Movie Clip, we can have greater control than if we loaded it into the main movie.

We then declare a new variable `audioBytesTotal` to equal the total size of the Movie Clip `audioloaded` by activating the script `getBytesTotal`. This is a Flash 5–only script that returns the size, in bytes, of the specified Movie Clip object. In this case, it basically returns the size of the external SWF.

We have captured values, but are currently doing nothing with it. At this stage in the speaker animation, we simply have the text `audio loading` fading on and off the button while the audio loads. Later in the timeline of the Speaker Movie Clip, we check whether the external audio has loaded with the following script:

```
audioBytesLoaded = audioloaded.getBytesLoaded();
if (audioBytesLoaded>=audioBytesTotal) {
  gotoAndPlay ("loud");
} else {
  gotoAndPlay ("loading2");
}
```

We are at the end of the "audio loading" speaker animation and need to determine whether the audio has loaded (so that we can start playing it) or whether we need to continue to load and loop the loading animation.

In the first line of the script, we declare another variable that measures the bytes of the external audio file that have loaded with the Flash 5–only script `getBytesLoaded`. It is now time to compare the number of bytes loaded versus the total number of bytes. A simple math formula compares the two. If `audioBytesLoaded` is equal to or greater than the `audioBytesTotal`, Flash should jump to the frame labeled `loud`. At this frame, we start playing the audio, remove the audio loading animation, and play the animation of the sound waves emulating from the speaker.

This effective piece of Flash 5 scripting did the trick. Check it out on our live site or on the enclosed CD.

Securing the Client Area

When working with clients on projects, we often need to post secure documents for review or sample pieces of projects we are currently working on. It is easy enough just to post this information on an FTP site and give the client a username and password, or just post an HTML project page that has no security but is hidden.

Our clients, as well as most other people, are used to being able to go to their Internet solution provider's Web site and log in to view these documents. We wanted to provide the same feature on the Flash site and use this opportunity to improve on the device we built for Design Mentor.

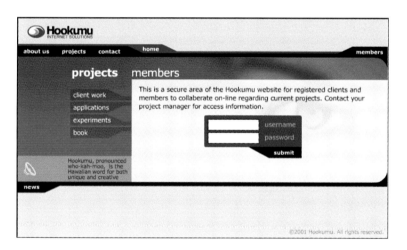

Figure 4.15 *The front gate.*

We knew that, over time, we would be adding a number of users to the secure area of the site. Those users would include our employees or contractors working on the project and the people to whom the client wanted to grant access. We decided we needed to do a little thinking ahead and some planning before executing the development of the secure area.

We identified the three main components of this system: the front gate, the master access list, and the secure area itself. Knowing that this system could eventually grow quickly, but not in the next few months, we made a couple of time-saving decisions.

First, we determined that, for now, all the username and passwords would exist in one secure file. This would be easy enough to build and control up-front, and would allow us relatively moderate growth over the next six months. The other approach we considered was the development of a simple database that would provide us with more robust user management tools.

Some user management tools that a database would allow us would be the ability to quickly add and delete users without needing to work in Flash. To do this, we would simply tell Flash that if the database did not return a correct username and password match, it should present the user with an error screen.

The database would also allow us to easily sort through the list of users, and could contain additional information related to the user, such as the project the user is associated with, the level of access the user has, and contact information.

Our advanced user management tool is built in a SQL 7 database that has very robust capabilities. For those of you familiar with this technology, you will realize that this is overkill for the type of traffic that Hookumu receives. However, our guys already know how to use it, and why drive a Yugo when you have a Ferrari in the garage.

For this type of functionality, there are many easy-to-learn database technologies that would provide the same features at a fraction of the cost and learning curve. Some of these include FileMaker Pro, Microsoft Access, or even a simple Excel spreadsheet that is really just a small database.

The final component of our secure area is the secure area itself. This is just another section of the Web site that is restricted from the anonymous user. The ultimate level of security in this situation would be to direct the user to an entirely new SWF file. This would be very secure, but it would require a bit more advanced scripting to identify the authenticated user as he jumped back and forth from the secure site to the public site, and not require him to log in each time.

In this case, we weren't protecting Fort Knox, so we opted to implement minimal, yet effective, countermeasures. When the user successfully logged in, we redirected him to an independent scene in the main SWF. When publishing the site in Flash, we also disabled "enable menu commands." This prevents users from right-clicking or Shift-clicking to get the menu that would allow them to step forward frame-by-frame until they reach the secure area. One additional security measure I recommend is to follow the general rule that only general comments and low-sensitivity information be contained in the actual Flash file. All other information—such as Microsoft Project files, Word documents, and Excel spreadsheets—should be kept as external files downloaded via the Flash site, and should also have file-level security.

Now that you understand the general architecture, let's discuss the details of how we built it. All the usernames and passwords for access to the secure area of the **site are** contained in an external text file. In the first frame of the preloader scene, we tell Flash to load this text file into the root of the movie with the following script:

```
loadVariablesNum ("members.txt", 0);
```

This says to load the external file onto the root of the movie at level 0. In Flash, you can load external elements into levels to keep track of them. Because this solution is simple, we just loaded it into level o. Within the text file, we have a list of usernames and passwords and we keep track of user counts. Here is a sample of what that text file looks like:

```
userCount=4&username0=creative&password0=unique&frame0=
creative&username1=lego&password1=buildit&frame1=
➥lego&username2=phil&password2=feeo&frame2=
➥phil&username3=steve
➥&password3=hookumu&frame3=
➥steve&DONE=1&
```

First, you should know that ampersands (&) are used to separate variables. Our first declaration, userCount, obviously tells Flash how many users this text file handles. Here we are indicating 4. The first is user o, with a username of creative and a password of unique. The frame label of creative refers to a frame label that we will use to access their secure content. These variables are repeated until we're done. We then indicate we are done (&DONE) so that Flash can stop thinking about this file.

Of course, this is transparent to the user. The first thing the user sees is the front gate. As mentioned earlier, this is just your standard log in screen. Both the username and password are simply input text fields that have variables assigned to them. The submit button handles all the action with the following script:

```
on (release, keyPress "<Enter>") {
  num = 0;
  if ((username eq "") or (password eq "")) {
    alert = "User name and password are required fields,
    ➥please try again.";
  } else if ((username ne "") or (password ne "")) {
    tellTarget ("tester") {
      gotoAndPlay (2);
    }
  }
}
```

Let's step through this simple script. The first line says that when the user clicks the submit button with the mouse or presses Enter, set a variable `num` to equal 0. We look to this variable later to see whether the user has already logged in so she doesn't have to authenticate every time she goes from Hookumu.com public pages to Hookumu.com secure pages. I will discuss this in detail in a moment.

The next line says that if the user is trying to click the submit button without filling in the appropriate fields, post the message `User name and password are required fields, please try again.`

The next line says if the username or password fields actually have something in them, tell the Movie Clip named `tester` to go into action. This Movie Clip is positioned off the visible stage and contains scripts that work the authentication.

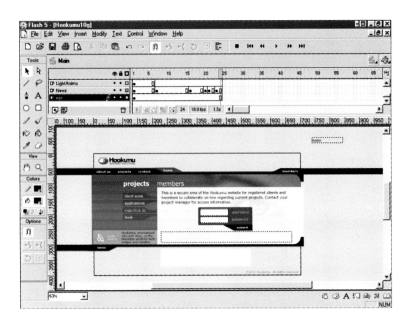

Figure 4.16 *Login screens and hidden* `tester` *MC.*

I should quickly note that the ne operator has been deprecated in Flash 5, and use of the new != (not equal) operator is recommended. I also recommended that eq be replaced with ++ (equality). I never said we were perfect, we just reverted to the methods we were used to. Having said that, we have since had our team go through the project and update all the scripting to the latest syntax.

On to the tester MC object. The top layer of the Tester Movie Clip contains frame scripts that will be used to authenticate users. Frame 1 simply sets the num variable to 0, and stops until the user enters something in the username and password fields and clicks Submit, which tells tester to go to frame 2 and play.

In frame 2, tester runs the following code:

```
testUser = "/:username"+/:num;
testPassword = "/:password"+/:num;
frame = eval("/:frame"+/:num);
/:frame = frame;
if ((/:username eq eval(testUser)) and (/:password eq
➥eval(testPassword))) {
  /:alert = "";
  tellTarget ("/") {
    gotoAndStop ("Members", /:frame);
  }
  gotoAndStop (1);
}
```

Line 1 declares a new variable, testUser, and tells it to equal a string created by taking the value of the username variable from the root timeline (what the user has just typed in) plus the variable num, which is currently 0. The num variable identifies which username and password in the text file to compare with the information the user just typed in. In line 2, we declare a second variable, testPassword, and tell it to equal a dynamic value of the root timeline variable password plus the variable num as well. In line 3, we declare a third variable, frame, and tell it to equal the sum of the main timeline variables `frame` (which is declared here and told to reside at the root level of the movie) and `num` (which would now equal `0`). We determine what these are by using the `eval` expression, which is Flash 5–compliant only, unless you use slash notations, and only evaluate variables. You should note that `/:` is equal to `_root:`, but has been deprecated in Flash 5. We now stay current on deprecated code, but at the time, we used `:/` simply because it was what we were used to and quicker to type than `_root:`.

The next line tells the main timeline variable `frame` to equal the new value we have assigned to the variable `frame` in the `tester` Movie Clip. This ensures that the two are continuously in sync Now that we've declared everything except independence, we can start working with the values.

In the next line of script, we say that if the value of the root variable `username` equals the value of `testuser` and the value of the root variable password equals the value of `testpassword`, tell the main timeline to go to the scene `Members` and the associated frame label. This allows us simply to update the text file when we create new users, and to give them a frame label in the `Members` scene where we can post their information.

This can get a little confusing. The important piece to remember is that the `username` and `password` variables are in this format: username0, username1, password0, password1, and so on. Even though the user enters unique information for his username and password, we verify this information against the text file and then use the formats I just listed.

Finally, I need to cover the handling of users who do not successfully authenticate. Up to this point, the site would simply sit there until the correct information is submitted. We wanted a more sophisticated manner to handle errors.

Figure 4.17   *Beyond the gate.*

If no match is found through the number of users listed in the text file, the user is sent to frame four of the `tester` MC, where we display an error message and reset the `num` value to 0 with the following script:

```
/:alert = "We are sorry we could not find your log-in
➥information. Please reenter your username and password
➥or contact your Project Manager for further
➥assistance.";
/:num = 0;
stop ();
```

This posts the error message on the screen and resets the `num` value to zero so that it is ready to test the next entry. As with most of our solutions, this is simple and effective. We tested this solution and found it to work with no errors other than the fact that we weren't able to enter the username and tab to the password field. In Flash, the Tab key takes you to the next interactive element in a list.

This could be a visible or invisible button or an input text field. The order determined is based on the level on which the element exists. Each element is on its own individual level, and unless you identify which level each element is on, it can be difficult to control the order.

To overcome this, we added the following script to the login frame:

```
next = "username";
Selection.setFocus(next);
```

Again we are declaring a variable `next` to equal `username`. We then use a piece of Flash 5—only ActionScript that tells the variable field `username` to be the focus of the screen. Meaning that when the user enters the frame, this field is active. If the user starts typing, what he types will appear in this field.

We then placed an invisible Movie Clip off the main stage with the following script:

```
on (keyPress "<Tab>") {
  if (next eq "password") {
    next = "username";
  } else if (next eq "username") {
    next = "password";
  }
  Selection.setFocus(next);
}
```

This simple code says that if the variable `next` equals `password` (which it currently does not), set the focus to the `username` field when the user presses the Tab key. If the variable `next` equals `username`, which in this case it currently does, jump to `password` when the user presses Tab. The last line—`Selection.setFocus(next)`—simply ensures that the focus follows where the user tabs.

Finally, we wanted to provide the user with a means to log off. Although this isn't really necessary because different users can't gain access to the same information, it does give a level of confidence to the user. In this case, the log-off button simply clears the `username` and `password` variables. If the user tries to gain access to a secure page, he will not be allowed in without re-authenticating.

Log-off buttons are helpful when working with sensitive files. I know I like to log off my online financials such as banking, investments, and online shopping. Better to be safe than sorry.

Scrolling

For Hookumu.com, we wanted most of the textual content to be loaded from an external file to enable a basic content management system. The company is growing and although we have several experienced Flash professionals, we wanted to enable our entire team to update the site easily. We implemented a solution similar to the one for DesignMentor.com, in which the majority of the textual content resides in external .TXT files.

This approach required us to integrate a scroll bar feature to allow for large quantities of text. The scroll bars for DesignMentor.com would have been sufficient and have to date been foolproof for the client. However, we wanted to see whether we could increase performance. For Design Mentor, we were limited by the use of Flash 4. But because Hookumu.com was being built in Flash 5, we felt we could improve on our scroll bar design.

Our plan, at the time, was to spend a couple of days writing a Flash 5 scroll bar solution that could be repurposed for future projects. However, before we dove into scripting, I decided to explore the various resources available to Flash developers. My hope was to learn enough from others' experiences not to be forced to start from scratch.

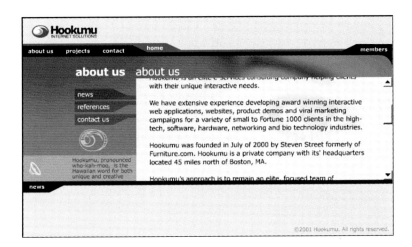

Figure 4.18 *Scrolling, scrolling, scrolling, get that content scrolling.*

I can't stress enough how important it is to take this step on any task. At Flashkit.com, I found a great source file from a gentleman named Thiago dos Santos Prado that did almost everything we required—which was basically to mimic the Windows scroll bars that most users are accustomed to. We wanted the scroll bars to be able to operate from a click of the arrow buttons at the top and bottom, by clicking in the gray area between the handle and the arrows, or by grabbing the handle and moving it. In addition, we wanted click or click-and-hold functionality, plus the added intelligence of scaling the handle based on the length of the scroll required. And we wanted all this to operate as efficiently as scroll bars do on browsers—but in Flash!

Thiago's Smart Clip solution did all this and used clip parameters that made our job even easier. *Clip parameters* are basically variables with values. They allow you, the Flash author, simply to use the Clip Parameters panel to modify these variables to control the functionality of that particular clip. Using clip parameters is not that difficult and allows for maximum flexibility and scalability when reusing clips. In this case, the clip parameters allowed us to control the amount of scroll that each bar had and the size of the handle without having to change it manually in the ActionScripting.

We were very excited to have found this solution, but a few challenges did present themselves. First was the concern of copyright. Were we allowed to use these scroll bars for our own use? That's the beauty of the Flash community. Flash developers are always posting solutions with source files attached for other developers to use and learn from.

The second challenge was that the artwork for the scroll bars didn't work with our design. This, too, was overcome quite easily. We simply replaced each button in Thiago's solution with a design of our own.

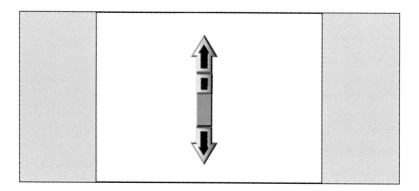

Figure 4.19 *Cool design from Thiago's original Scroll Bar.*

The final challenge we encountered was by far the largest. All of Thiago's code was written in Portuguese! None of us could read or write Portuguese, so we thought we were in trouble. However, after some quick investigation, we found that this would not be an issue for use on Hookumu.com or future solutions. Thiago included a very thorough read me file in English. However, for this book and for our own knowledge and better understanding of the code, we wanted to grasp what some of the more complex scripting was doing. Luckily enough, Thiago was willing to translate and document the various components.

I would like to walk you through the major components, but keep in mind that much of this is in Portuguese, and I don't think we want to start giving foreign language lessons! Instead, I recommend that you review the ActionScripting code in the source file on the accompanied CD-ROM, and refer to the next few paragraphs where I will translate and explain the various variables.

The main functionality of the scroll bars exists within the first frame of the main scroll bar Movie Clip called `clip_barra_rolagem`. You should notice in the Library that the icon for this Movie Clip is a bit different than other Movie Clips. This is because this particular Movie Clip has been made a *Smart Clip*, which is just a Movie Clip with clip parameters associated with it. The icon is a helpful indicator when organizing the elements of a complex solution.

The script in the first frame of the `clip_barra_rolagem` Smart Clip begins with

```
inicializar();
stop();
```

This is the initialize function that is called as soon as scrolling starts. The `inicializar()` function is as follows:

```
function inicializar()
{
        y_inicial_rolagem = rolagem._y;

        pos_inicial_clip = direcao == "vertical" ?
    ➥eval("_parent." + clip_associado)._y :
    ➥eval("_parent." + clip_associado)._x;

        atualizar_rolagem = true;

        inicializado = true;
}
```

The first line, `y_inicial_rolagem`, tells us where the moving bar is when all the action starts. The next line, `pos_inicial_clip`, saves the initial position of the associated Movie Clip that is being moved. The statement `atualizar_rolagem = true` forces the operations to refresh and recalculate the operations. The `inicializado` variable looks to see whether this function has been called.

```
 1: ajustar_limite_pos()
 2: pos_atual
 3: deslocamento_max
 4: deslizar_baixo()
 5: deslizar_cima()
 6: atualizacao_automatica()
 7: tratar_deslocamento_rapido()
 8: pressionado_cima
 9: pressionado_baixo
10: cont_baixo and cont_cima
11: ajustar_tamanho_rolagem()
```

Line 1 is called to guarantee that the moving bar is restricted to the Y direction, and in line 2 this function indicates the current positive location of the Movie Clip. Line 3 is translated as *max-moving*; this variable saves how far the clip can be moved in pixels.

In line 4, this function can be translated as `moving_down()`, and is called to perform the moving of the moving bar and of the associated clip down. The movement is performed by changing the value of the variable `pos_atual` (or `currently_pos`). Line 5 can be translated as `moving_up()`, and is the opposite of the earlier `moving_down()` function. After all, what goes up, must come down.

The next line can be translated as `automatic_refresh()`, and is called by the clip event `enterFrame()`. Line 6 translates as `fast_moving_handle()`, and is called when the user presses (and keeps pressed) the mouse button on the up/down scroll bar button.

Line 7 checks whether the user is clicking on the up button and translates as `up_pressed`. Line 8 is similar to the preceding function; this checks whether the user is clicking on the down button and translates as `down_pressed`.

`cont_down` and `cont_up` are counters that mark whether the user is pressing long enough to switch from single-click scrolling to fast and smooth continuous scrolling. Line 11 can be translated as `adjust_moving_bar_sized()`, and calculates the size of the moving bar as a percent rate of the entire scroll. The percent rate is calculated by this division: `fator_deslocamento` / `deslocamento_max` or `each_click_moving` / `max_moving`.

I'm sure that I have butchered much of the translation, but in that is the beauty of ActionScripting: No matter what you call them, they are still variables and they function no matter what the actual words say.

If you followed the scroll bars we used for Design Mentor in Chapter 3, "DesignMentor.com," this should not be a huge jump to follow. I would like to thank Thiago for the generous use of his code. Not only did his code allow us to quickly implement smooth scroll bars in our site, but also he allowed us to talk about them in this book.

Final Touches

After we had most of the elements complete and were in the final stages of look-and-feel development, we needed to address the plug-in detection and pre-loader for the site.

The Web site is Flash 5–compatible only because this afforded us a great deal of flexibility in the design and scripting of the many site features. However it actually presented a problem with the Flash 4 plug-in. Flash 4 is capable of displaying Flash 5 content until it needs to interpret a script or effect it does not understand, and then it tends to hang up and appear broken.

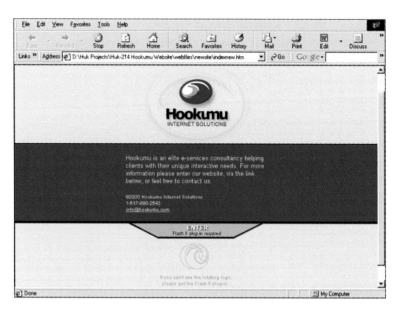

Figure 4.20   *Detecting the Flash 5 plug-in.*

Because most users wouldn't know which plug-in they have, we had to assume that they would not bother to check and would just try to enter the site. After all, that is what I would do. If it didn't work, I might go get the latest plug-in, but most likely I would just forget about the Web site and go somewhere else. We didn't want that to happen; after all, we are supposed to know what we are doing. This meant we had to detect whether users have version 5 of the plug-in, and if not, make it apparent to them and give them the devices to go get the latest one.

Our first step was to handle those users who had Flash version 3.0 or earlier, or no plug-in at all. Imagine! In the HTML page, we placed a small, rotating 3D Hookumu logo (more on that later). If the users didn't have the plug-in, they would see the broken puzzle icon with a message in HTML below it that tells them they need to get the latest Flash plug-in. The message also directs them to the appropriate page on Macromedia.com to download the plug-in.

Users could still try to access the site and we decided there was no reason to prevent this because the effort to do so was not insignificant. Instead, we simply reinforced it by adding a small comment below the Enter button stating that the site required the latest plug-in. A good rule of thumb to use when designing for usability is always assume that your audience has no experience using Web sites. It might sound crazy, but it works! I'm sure that the folks at Amazon.com consider me an idiot when they design their interfaces, so their site has many devices built in to make my shopping and experience easy and simple.

So, our thinking was this: If the user has no plug-in or a plug-in earlier than version 4.0, and he ignores the broken puzzle icon *and* the statement asking him to get the latest plug-in *and* the statement below the Enter button, just let him do what he wants as he will most likely anyway.

Our bigger concern was with those users who have Flash version 4.0, but either think they have version 5 or just don't know. Because the Flash 4 plug-in will let them into the site initially, it quickly makes our site appear as though it's broken. We couldn't afford that.

What we did was build a small detection device into the looping Flash 3D Hookumu logo on the HTML entrance page. We started, again, with a solution we found on Flashkit.com, and modified it to meet our needs. I have been unable to locate the creator, so if you know him or her, please let me know. The following is the code and how it works.

In the first frame of the main timeline of the `LogoSpin.fla`, we put the following script:

```
playerVersion = eval("$version");
```

This defines the user's plug-in version and stores it in a new variable called `playerVersion`.

```
myLength = length(playerVersion);
```

181

This script uses the `length` function to identify the number of characters in the variable `playerVersion` and stores it in the new variable `myLength`.

```
while (i<=myLength) {
  i = i+1;
  temp = substring(playerVersion, i, 1);
  if (temp eq " ") {
    platform = substring(playerVersion, 1, i-1);
    majorVersion = substring(playerVersion, i+1, 1);
    secondHalf = substring(playerVersion, i+1,
    ➥myLength-i);
    minorVersion = substring(secondHalf, 5, 2);
  }
}
```

This whole script uses a looping check to determine the version number of the user's plug-in. Because the plug-in version is a series of major numbers and minor numbers, such as version 4.051, we need to use this information to determine exactly which plug-in the user has.

```
if (majorVersion>=4) {
```

Because `$version` was not available in the first releases of Flash 4, this script will check for that. This states that the user has version 4.0 or later, or release 11 or later.

```
} else {
  majorVersion = "4";
}
```

This states that the user has version 4.0 or later, or release 10 or earlier.

```
if (majorVersion eq "4") {
  gotoAndStop (2);
} else if (majorVersion eq "5") {
  // Send the user to a Flash 5 page
  gotoAndPlay (3);
}
```

Here we use all the preceding information either to send the user to frame 2 and display an error message if he does not have Flash 5 or, if he has Flash 5, to send him to frame 3 where we start to play a looping and spinning Hookumu logo.

There are at least two-dozen ways to go about doing this. The important factor is controlling the users' experience so they do not encounter errors trying to see a Flash 5 solution with a version 4.0 plug-in.

Post-Mortem

All in all, we have received great reviews on the Hookumu.com site and it continues to meet our needs and the needs of our clients and partners. I recommend that you review the source file on the CD-ROM of the site because a great deal is taking place that I did not write about in the book.

Since this book was written, we have made some changes to the site. For user management in the secure area, we now implement a more dynamic and secure component that contains user information in a SQL 7 database. To enter user information, we have an HTML interface that imports and updates the database. In our main Flash file, we implemented a Generator object that looks to this database and whenever it encounters a new user, it creates an area for the user in the main SWF. We had to implement some workarounds to make it entirely dynamic with no Flash authoring required to create new user areas. It was a lot of work, but this will serve as a component of some products we are prototyping as well as solutions for new clients that want Flash-based user management.

With the early solution, we ran into the challenge of keeping the user authenticated after he logged in. To tackle this late in the game (and without extending the deadline), we decided that after the user logged in unsuccessfully, we would display the user's username and password in the appropriate login fields. That way, if the user went back to the public site, surfed around, and then returned to the members' area, all he would have to do is click the submit button again and he could get right in. This was not ideal, but it worked.

In our next release, we trapped this information in an external file. When users come to the login screen, we look to this file and if the user has logged in, we pass those values along and seamlessly move the user to the appropriate secure area. To prevent security from traveling from user to user, we dump this information every 30 minutes, or as necessary. Another way we could have accomplished this would have been to set an actual session cookie on the user's machine and checked against this. *Cookies* are temporary Internet files in which you can store data. A *session cookie* is data that is stored only as long as the user is in this session of Web browsing. After a period of time or when the user quits the browser, the data and the cookie, are dumped.

For the secure client area, try logging in as `Lego` with a password of `buildit`. It is a great Flash piece and the case study for the next chapter.

CHAPTER

LEGO Build It Prototype

ADVANCED

LEGO building blocks.

Overview

Identifying potential new clients, prototyping, layering of duplicated Movie Clips, tracking objects, and keeping it simple. I will discuss all these in this chapter as I take you through the story of how Hookumu decided we wanted LEGO as a client and developed a prototype to attract their attention.

Using Flash 5, Swift 3d for vector-based LEGO blocks, and a one-scene, one-frame timeline, we created a layered-based, drag-and-drop game that lets users build their own creations. It also allowed us, the developers, to track the blocks as we were prototyping.

The Players

All the chapters so far have dealt with stories involving clients who had some need that we were able to address with a Flash solution. In my experience, this is usually how business is conducted in the interactive industry.

However, as a business owner and leader, I have learned that the clients are not always sitting around waiting for our services. Often times we can find ourselves in a position in which we are ready for the next project and there is nothing for us to work on.

At Hookumu, we call this "the peaks and valleys business cycle." I believe this is the nature of our business as most projects never see the fifth month because clients are always in a rush to get Internet and interactive solutions out the door in three or four months. When your company is between projects or as projects are winding down, everybody starts to investigate new leads and you basically get the word out on the street that you have room for a new project. In this way, we often find ourselves working with three or four new clients.

Over the next few weeks, we start to turn these opportunities into actual projects. Sometimes all the opportunities demand your attention because the clients want actual work developed. Before you know it, you are at the peak. Everybody is busy working on too many projects and nobody is thinking about business development.

A couple of months go by, and as the projects near completion, you start to realize that there is no work in the pipeline: You are now in a valley. Hopefully, over time, you get better at this and the peaks and valleys become rolling hills with a few comfortable plateaus.

I'm writing about this because I think this is a critical piece of the interactive story. Not all projects can just land in your lap. With larger and more prestigious accounts, you often have to take the first step. I wanted to have one chapter of the book talk about prototyping and proactively selling a client who might not yet realize it has a need. This is how I believed Hookumu could get larger clients.

At Hookumu, we had landed a couple of interesting new accounts and Phil Stephenson had recently joined our team.

The new projects were keeping us busy, but I had my eye on the next valley. Phil was a great addition to the team, and I wanted to maximize our combined talents by landing an account that would challenge our skills and add a recognizable company to our client list.

With no limits to the company we could work with, we started to explore. A few of the first companies that came to mind included Disney, AOL, and Microsoft. We investigated each and determined that the politics and red tape at these companies didn't make them likely candidates for our first big-name client. To work with AOL, you need to first submit a request in writing, and then wait. Microsoft requires you to be a partner, and Disney does a great deal of its work in-house. Eventually, we set our sights on the LEGO Group. LEGO.com is based in New York City, which is close to Hookumu and although it has an amazing in-house development team, the company does work with vendors.

LEGO has a very powerful and recognizable brand; after all, everyone has played with LEGO bricks at one point or another in his or her life. It really was a no-brainer to see how the Internet and Flash were a great match for the types of products that LEGO markets.

Figure 5.1   *The LEGO brand.*

We quickly set off to review the Web site and discovered that the LEGO Group has done an excellent job of developing an online presence of its brand. All the better, we thought. When you look at the site, you think LEGO: It's highly interactive, it's fun, entertaining, and there are elements everywhere that beg you to explore and build. On top of that, a great deal of the site has been built in Flash!

Figure 5.2 *LEGO.com.*

We were very excited because we were confident that with our unique Flash experience and back-end expertise, LEGO would quickly want to involve us in its future projects. Our true task was to figure out a way to attract the company's attention. It was tempting to run to Outlook or the phone and let the folks at LEGO know that we existed so that the projects would start rolling. However, we also realized that this was unrealistic. After all, the company must get calls like that everyday, and I'm sure that the company has vendors in place to do much of the work.

We needed to capture their attention with an interactive Flash solution that would show them that we possessed a unique combination of talents. We wanted to invest a minimal amount of effort that would produce the greatest return: ultimately, a project for LEGO.

We felt the project had to be done in Flash. It had to be simple enough that we could build it quickly, yet also be complex enough that it would be something they didn't currently have on their site or something they could quickly reproduce.

The Client's Need: Hookumu Business Development

At this point, Hookumu was still made up of just Phil and myself with three contractors handling some light design and production work. The plan was to use our unique skills to land LEGO to grow the business. After minimal exploration, we decided to create a simple drag-and-drop building block application. Similar to the basic first blocks LEGO had when I was a kid, this application would give users the ability to select from six basic shapes in a variety of colors, and drag the shape to a main green baseboard where they could begin building whatever their imagination wanted. The basic concept was a game. Although there was no winning, the goal of this game was to simulate the experience kids have when playing with LEGOs: letting imagination lead the way.

The Solution

We felt the solution was core to LEGO's brand and would add true benefit and fun for the users. At the same time, it would showcase some of our skills because we had never seen anything like this on the Web before.

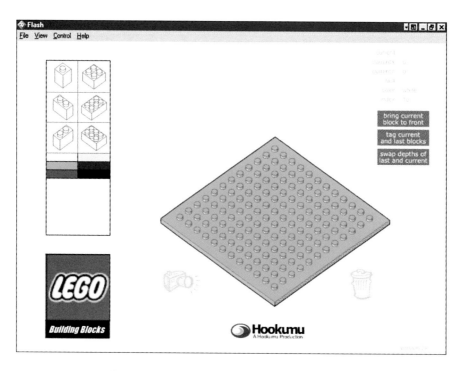

Figure 5.3 *The final solution.*

Building the Basic Blocks

I first started with the design of the interface elements. I wanted the entire solution to be easy to create and for the end user to use. Allowing users to build with and stack blocks would be easy to build if we showed the blocks from a side angle, but it wouldn't be very fun to use Tetris-like, 2D-only shapes. On the other hand, it would have been a far larger and more difficult undertaking to create a 3D version with perspectives and rotating capabilities. This also might have proven to be too complex for the end user to work with to be fun. We decided on the middle ground: an orthographic view of the workspace.

Orthographic is a term I learned doing 3D development. It means a view with no perspective. There's no horizon line, so no lines converge. This was perfect for our solution because we were dealing with basic block shapes. An orthographic perspective would mean that we could develop a fixed number of shapes, and they would work regardless of where the user placed them on the workspace.

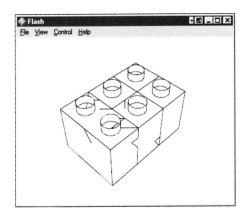

Figure 5.4   *A building block with perspective.*

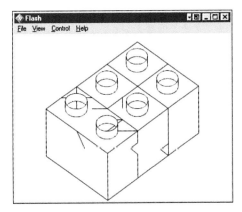

Figure 5.5   *A building block in an orthographic view.*

The key to keeping the view orthographic and removing any perspective was to place the camera as far away as possible. By doing so, there is no detectable perspective.

If the camera were extremely close, the perspective would be extreme and the blocks would never look correct when they were placed together.

We explored a variety of ways to create the shapes. At first, we thought we could easily create them in FreeHand with the perspective grid. We designed a couple of blocks this way, but we quickly realized that we had to have exact control over block placement in the Flash application because we were dealing with blocks that snap together and there are only a few ways that these blocks can sit. The shapes would be snapping to a grid controlled via ActionScripting.

It is possible to create the precise block shapes in FreeHand or Illustrator, but I wasn't confident that the snap-to grid would be precise after 10 or so blocks were linked back to back. I wanted to find a better way to build the blocks. I first determined that the lowest common denominator in all the blocks is the single cap block.

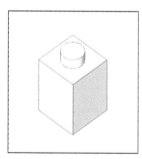

Figure 5.6   *The lowest common denominator.*

We started by creating the body of the single cap block from a simple shape that's nearly square, but taller. Because this was the starting point for both the grid and all the blocks, it wasn't necessary for it to be of any particular size other than geometrically square from the top view. The cap is simply an extruded circle. We built both the square and the extruded circle directly in our 3D program Strata Studio Pro. Because the shapes were so simple this was accomplished quickly with little effort or errors. From Strata, we used our typical process, which was mentioned in previous chapters: Export as a DXF file, and use the Crossroads utility to convert the DXF's into .3ds files for import into Swift and then into SWFs for Flash. Whew, that sounds like a lot of steps! It is fast, though.

We now had to create the remaining blocks and I came up with a simple, yet effective, means of doing so. In Strata, we simply put a series of single cap blocks together to create our other shapes. Two blocks together created our two-cap shape; four blocks together created the square four-cap shape, and so on. Strata provides the tools to precisely snap the shapes to each other so that the distances remain consistent. We then exported the groups and in Flash removed the interior lines so that we had only the larger shape and no longer a group of the smaller blocks. Not only did this keep the shapes precise without having to do any exact calculations that would risk error, but it provided us the plan for creating the grid as well.

Until this point, we were strictly working with the wireframes in Flash. Color is an element independent of the 3D shape, and I'll discuss it in a moment.

Remember the large green floors that LEGO used to give you in all their kits? We called this the grid and to build it we simply lined up 144 (twelve by twelve) of the single cap shapes. By lining them up edge to edge, viewing them with edges only and no fills, and zooming in closely, we were able to get each shape precisely lined up, with at least enough precision for this solution. We then broke apart the shapes so that we were left with only the 144 base Movie Clips and 144 cap Movie Clips. Finally, we deleted all the base blocks, leaving behind only the caps. Because all the shapes started with the single cap shape, we had a precise grid. We then just created a wide and long base for the

144-cap grid and colored this base block green. The grid would never change or move so we could generate this by eye and not have to start in 3D.

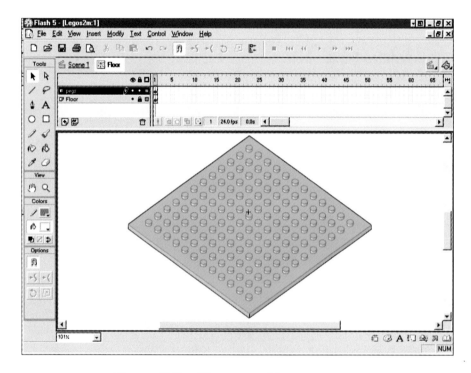

Figure 5.7 *The green grid.*

Square Off Them Blocks, Mister!

Now that we had all our basic shapes in Flash, it was time to add highlights and optimize file size. The cap is obviously one single shape used over and over to create four shapes: single-cap, two-cap, four-cap, and six-cap. We didn't want to invest time in creating shapes that could be rotated for a solution we didn't even have a client for; we thought there was a better way to handle rotation. By fixing the user's view to the orthographic isometric point of view, we ended up with only two shapes that we needed to provide two angles for. Every other shape was identical from

every angle you could see in our project. Think about it:
The single- and four-cap shapes look the same from any
angle in our current view. The two-cap and six-cap shapes
have only two possible views from our camera angle, and
these are created from one block outline symbol. This
meant that we needed only four basic shape outlines and
one cap. Very small.

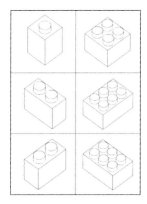

Figure 5.8 *The basic shapes.*

The final design element that needed to be developed was
the highlights on each of the shapes. Without the
highlights, the blocks didn't feel 3D enough and looked flat.
Because we didn't want to create a unique shape for every
color block, we built the blocks in Flash as a series of
shapes and layers.

Each of the final six shapes is composed of four layers. The
top layer is the cap, and the next layer down is just the
outline of the shape. There are three sides to each block:
left, right, and top. Each side has its own color cast. The
top is the pure color used. The left side is slightly brighter,
and the right is slightly darker. Because ActionScripting
would generate the colors dynamically, we put two shapes
on the third layer—one each for the left and right sides of
the block that we filled with highlight and shade colors.
By putting a 30% Alpha effect on those shapes, they would

simply lighten and darken the color they were over, regardless of what that color was.

The bottom layer, called color, simply contains the overall shape of the block we happen to be looking at. We gave this shape an instance name so that we could use ActionScripting to apply color to it from anywhere in the movie. More on this later as we step through the code. A benefit of this design is that the camera angle is such that we didn't need to create a separate color shape just for the caps because they were within the color areas.

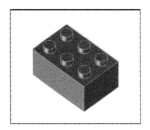

Figure 5.9   *Shapes with highlights.*

Pick a Block, Any Block

When the user first launches Lego Building Blocks, there is only one thing she can do: Select a block from the block selector panel. We wanted to keep the user interface as simple to use as possible, so we developed a three-step process: pick a block, pick a color, and then use it.

In general, the block selector panel has three sets of blocks. First is the upper wireframe blocks that the user auditions for use. These have invisible buttons over them that I will discuss in a moment. Below the wireframe blocks is a multi-block Movie Clip called blocks that appears as just the single cap block on the workspace. This is used to display the correct block as the user rolls over the wireframe blocks. Finally, the actual blocks that will be used for dragging are stacked on top of each other under the blocks Movie Clip. These are visible on the workspace, but when the movie runs, they are set to invisible until the user selects a block. More on this in a minute.

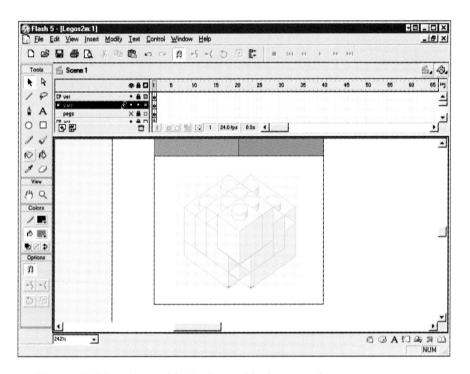

Figure 5.10 *Here a block, there a block, everywhere a block-block.*

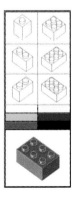

Figure 5.11 *Block selector panel.*

First, the user rolls over one of the six basic, white building blocks. As they roll over a block, it appears in the active block window below the color selector.

Over each of the blocks in the block selector panel is an invisible button that contains the following scripting:

```
on (rollOver) {
  tellTarget ("blocks") {
    gotoAndPlay ("block1");
  }
}
```

blocks is an instance of a Movie Clip that resides in the active block window. This Movie Clip contains all the blocks in the block selector panel. The line gotoAndPlay ("block1"); refers to the frame label in the blocks MC that corresponds to the frame at which the appropriate block is located, so when you roll over the button, the correct block shows in the active block window. "block1" changes depending on which block you roll over.

Frame 1 of blocks has an invisible single cap block for registration purposes that the user cannot see. The following script on each of the invisible buttons over the selection blocks makes it so that no block is displayed if the user rolls off the block selector panel.

```
on (releaseOutside, rollOut, dragOut) {
 tellTarget ("blocks") {
  gotoAndStop (1);
 }
}
```

The color selector in general updates all the blocks in the multi-block Movie Clip called blocks. Be careful, the terminology can be a little confusing. On rollover of the colors, it changes the colors temporarily, but always goes back to the chosen color as defined by the variable color on rolloff. The color variable is set on release of the color button.

Each block has a number associated with it, through the variable num. Clicking on the button tells the related block to be visible and stay that way. Now the user has selected a block, and it is visible and fixed in the active block window. The user can now view what the block would look like in one of six different colors.

```
on (release) {
 num = "1";
 setProperty ("_root.block1", _visible, "1");
 setProperty ("_root.block2", _visible, "0");
 setProperty ("_root.block3", _visible, "0");
 setProperty ("_root.block4", _visible, "0");
 setProperty ("_root.block5", _visible, "0");
 setProperty ("_root.block6", _visible, "0");
}
```

Over each color chooser block is the same invisible button with the following script, which, except for the color, is the same for all:

```
on (rollOver) {
 count = 1;
 while (count < 7) {
  tellTarget ("/block"+ count) {
   gotoAndStop ("white");
  }
  count = count + 1;
 }
}
```

The rollover tells all the blocks to go to the rolled-over color choice on the fly. Rolling over the color sets the variable count to 1 and then uses this variable to target a Movie Clip on the root timeline with the instance name of block+count which is located in the active block window. This Movie Clip is then told to go to the frame labeled white or whatever color the invisible button is on top of. It loops through all the numbers to repeat the process for all of the Movie Clips in the active block window. We could have accomplished the same effect with a series of `telltarget` commands that would tell each Movie Clip to go to the appropriate color when rolled over, but this would have required much more coding and technically would have been slower because of the extra scripting.

```
on (release) {
 count = 1;
 while (count < 7) {
  tellTarget ("/block"+ count) {
   gotoAndStop ("white");
  }
  count = count + 1;
 }
 color = "white";
}
```

When the user clicks the button, the variable `color` is, on release, set to the corresponding color. So, when the user rolls over any of the block picker buttons, the current color choice is shown. The user clicks and now the appropriate block—with the appropriate color—is shown within the active block window and is ready to be used.

```
on (rollOut, dragOut) {
 count = 1;
 while (count < 7) {
  tellTarget ("/block"+ count) {
   gotoAndStop (/:color);
  }
  count = count + 1;
 }
}
```

The rollout tells all the blocks to go back to the currently chosen color.

Watch Where You Put Those Blocks

At this point, the user has selected a block and a color she would like. It's now time to move the blocks onto the grid as the user starts building something.

In the active block window, the user sees the current block choice in its chosen color. On top of this block resides our famous invisible button with the following script:

```
on (press) {
  index = /:index + 1;
  duplicateMovieClip ("/block"+/:num, "block"+/:index,
/:index+1);
  tellTarget ("/block"+/:index) {
    gotoAndStop (/:color);
  }
  startDrag ("/block"+/:index, true);
  /:current = getProperty ( "/block"+/:index, _name );
}
```

When the user clicks and holds the mouse button on this button, the first line simply uses the index variable as a counter that will be used as we go along and will continue to increase. The second line duplicates the appropriate block by attaching the num variable (set when the user made it the active block) to block, and sets the new block's depth and new name. Then, we make sure that the block is the correct color with the line gotoAndStop (/:color);.

The next line starts dragging. The last line sets the variable current in the block Movie Clip so that we know which is the active block. I should mention that index is a running counter of the number of blocks the user has created. Each block that the user creates has an instance name of block plus a number added to it. In addition, we use index to control depth because you can't have more than one duplicated Movie Clip per layer. Setting the current block is used in conjunction with the "bring to front" and "depth swapping" functions to control which block is up front.

```
on (release, releaseOutside) {
  call ("_root.controller:release");
  stopDrag ();
}
```

When the user releases the mouse button, we call the frame labeled `release` in the controller Movie Clip (which I'll explain next). And, obviously, if we didn't put the last line in, the block would forever be stuck to the cursor.

In the upper-right corner of the workspace—off the stage— we have a small Movie Clip called `controller`. The controller is a device that universally tracks the first and last blocks that the user touched to maintain the depth of each block. It also contains some functions for trashing the blocks and the snap-to information for the grid. Here's how.

The following script is in frame 1:

```
/:currentX = getProperty("/"+/:current, _x);
/:currentY = getProperty("/"+/:current, _y);
/:lastX = getProperty("/"+/:last, _x);
/:lastY = getProperty("/"+/:last, _y);
```

Here we merely set some variables that continually check where the current and last blocks are; further explanation is coming.

The `release` frame contains several scripts. The first script is

```
// trash check
if ((/:currentX > 630) and (/:currentY > 430)) {
 removeMovieClip ("/"+/:current);
}
```

This script first checks the position of the block to see whether the user is trashing it. Basically, if the block is released to the right or below the X and Y of the upper-left corner of the trash can, the `removeMovieClip` statement removes the Movie Clip found in the `current` variable.

Here's the next script:

```
//
// limits check
//
```

```
setProperty ("/"+/:current, _x, 300 + ((int((/:currentX
- 300)/17)) * 17));
setProperty ("/"+/:current, _y, 2 + ((int((/:currentY -
2)/12)) * 12));
```

This piece performs the snap-to-grid for each block. It forces each block to sit on the predetermined grid. The X spacing is in increments of 17 and the Y is in increments of 12. The numbers 300 and 2 are simply where it needs to start counting to make it work. Notice that it's wrapped in parentheses after the word int, which just makes it an integer so that we don't have decimal points.

```
//

if (/:currentX <300) {
 setProperty ("/"+/:current, _x, "300");
} else if (/:currentX >670) {
 setProperty ("/"+/:current, _x, "670");
}
if (/:currentY <38) {
 setProperty ("/"+/:current, _y, "38");
} else if (/:currentY >458) {
 setProperty ("/"+/:current, _y, "458");
}
//
```

The last bit of coding in the release frame of the controller Movie Clip simply ensures that the pieces are dropped within the outer limits of the workspace. It's that easy, but let's step through it again.

Let's say that when the user releases the block it actually has an X value of 452.7. If we work from the outside of the parentheses in, we get 452.7 minus 300, which equals 152.7. 152.7 divided by 17 equals 8.982, which, as an integer, equals 8. 8 multiplied by 17 equals 136. 136 + 300 equals 436, which is on the grid, eight steps over from 300.

Within each of the block Movie Clips is an invisible button, masked to the shape of the block, which does a couple key things:

```
on (press) {
 /:last = /:current;
 /:current = getProperty ( "", _name );
 startDrag ("");
}
```

It first sets the `last` variable within the Movie Clip to the variable `current` from the root level. The variable `current` is then set to the name of the current block we are working with and starts the drag. This basically tells Flash which block is the current one and which is the last one, and then tells the current block to start dragging.

```
on (release, releaseOutside) {
 call ("_root.controller:release");
 stopDrag ();
}
```

When the user releases the block, the first line calls the controller Movie Clip and runs the release sequence, and then it stops dragging.

Shhhh, I'm Hunting Code

At this point in the project, we had enough of a prototype to put something in front of LEGO to get our idea across. However, we still had a couple of issues to resolve. Although it was not our intention to work out these issues before presenting the prototype to LEGO, I wanted to make sure that we had a firm grip on and understanding of them. I thought this would be a good learning opportunity.

We called these issues *the DEV stuff*. The DEV stuff consists of the tracking elements and buttons you see at the top right of the solution. The primary issue we wanted to understand better was how we would control the layering of each block on the workspace as users placed many shapes on the grid. In addition, we needed to implement a device that could dynamically track each block and its properties (such as color) as well as swap it to a different depth. It was critical that this happened behind the scenes and without the user's knowledge. To ensure that we understood it correctly, we put the tracking information on the workspace with the intention of removing it for the final solution. Here is how we did it.

This next bit of scripting ensures that when the user drops a block on the workspace, it is immediately brought to the forefront. We wrestled with many ways that we could handle block layering, and finally decided that we should treat this the way you work in the real world. In the real world, if you build a tower of LEGO blocks, you cannot remove the one in the middle without removing the blocks on top of it. We took the same approach by placing the most recent block at the forefront. You can find this on the "bring current block to front" button:

```
on (release) {
  index = /:index + 1;
  color = getProperty ( "/"+/:current, _currentframe );
  duplicateMovieClip ("/"+/:current, "block"+/:index,
  ➥index + 1);
  tellTarget ("block"+/:index) {
    gotoAndStop (/:color);
  }
  removeMovieClip ("/"+/:current);
}
```

The first line sets the index variable one higher. The next line tells us what color the current block is. The next line duplicates the current block, moves it to the highest depth, and renames it. The tellTarget Action is redundant, but it sets the right color, just in case. The removeMovieClip statement removes the old block as the new one is created. Keep in mind that this occurs within a split second. In all our reviews, it has yet to be detected.

The next bit of code tags what the last block was and what the current block is. This is helpful to know when the user starts to work with existing blocks on the workspace. We need to maintain depth checking and layering and here is how it is done.

```
/:last = /:current;
/:current = getProperty ( "", _name );
```

The following is the code we use for our developers' notes. This is used in several places; this one being located on the "tag current and last blocks" button. This code simply duplicates a balloon, brings it to the current mouse location, makes it visible, and starts a drag. It then puts the appropriate text inside the balloon. The final two lines of code remove the balloon when the user is done.

```
on (rollOver) {
  duplicateMovieClip ("bloon", "bloon2", index + 100);
  setProperty ("bloon2", _visible, "1");
  startDrag ("bloon2", true);
  bloon2:text = "DEV NOTE: Indicates which blocks are
  ➡current and last.";
}
on (releaseOutside, rollOut, dragOut) {
  removeMovieClip ("bloon2");
}
```

The rollover Action grabs the text balloon, or `bloon`, from off the workspace and tags the most active block.

```
on (press) {
  duplicateMovieClip ("CTag", "CTag1", 9999);
  setProperty ("CTag1", _x, currentX);
  setProperty ("CTag1", _y, currentY);
  duplicateMovieClip ("LTag", "LTag1", 9998);
  setProperty ("LTag1", _x, getProperty (last, _x ));
  setProperty ("LTag1", _y, getProperty (last, _y ));
}
```

This merely positions the current and last tags to the same position of the current and last block when the user clicks.

```
on (release) {
 removeMovieClip ("CTag1");
 removeMovieClip ("LTag1");
}
```

This gets rid of the tags when the user releases the mouse button.

```
on (release) {
 eval(/:current).swapDepths(eval(/:last));
```

This is very basic. It just swaps the depths of the current and last blocks. This is a basic function, but it is one that we can call as necessary to swap block depths if necessary. No device, other than the swap depth button, was put in place to enable this action, but we wanted to confirm the functionality.

The rest of the scripting pertains to the development balloons that appear as necessary to prove functionality. These would be removed for the final solution, but we showcased them to LEGO to prove that we were tracking actions within the project and could easily—although it would be labor-intensive—implement more advanced functionality.

```
on (rollOver) {
 duplicateMovieClip ("bloon", "bloon2", index + 100);
```

Again, this duplicates the bloon and puts it "higher" than any block.

```
 setProperty ("bloon2", _visible, "1");
```

This makes the bloon visible.

```
 startDrag ("bloon2", true);
```

This sets it a-draggin'.

```
bloon2:text = "DEV NOTE: Testing moving indiv block to
top Z layer.";
```

This tells what text to display in the bloon.

```
}
on (releaseOutside, rollOut, dragOut) {
 removeMovieClip ("bloon2");
}
```

Finally, this gets rid of the bloon.

Getting LEGO's Attention

We felt it was time to show the solution to our potential new client, and that was a feat in itself. We hadn't yet established a relationship with LEGO, and we weren't sure how our solution would be accepted. I started by researching the Web site, and with more effort than I anticipated, found out that although LEGO itself is headquartered in Denmark, the Web team is located in New York.

I also discovered, in the site search, a deeply hidden Just Build application that was similar to the one we just finished! Our initial reaction was one of concern over having lost an opportunity. We quickly learned, however, that the Just Build solution on the site utilized a 3D plug-in called Cult 3D. LEGO's Cult 3D version was impressive and offered some advanced solutions (such as the capability to rotate pieces) and also offered some uniquely shaped blocks that we did not.

However, the Just Build application also had some drawbacks, such as a heavy download for both the plug-in that most users would not have and the content itself, which was a bit cumbersome to interact with. We felt that there was enough of a difference and enough unique qualities of our solution to proceed with the hunt.

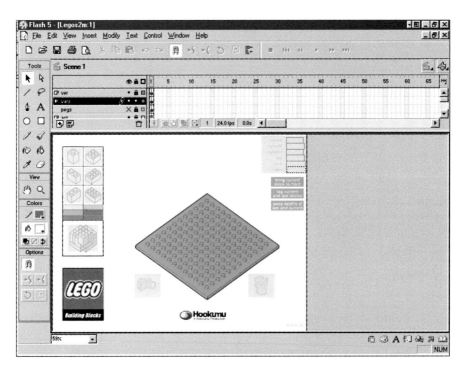

Figure 5.12   *The working Flash file.*

So, I posted all the necessary files on our Web site and set forth dialing the New York office phone number, where I reached the employee who happened to answer the phone. I explained that I had developed a prototype using LEGO's blocks to test the capabilities of Flash 5, and wanted to see what the interest level would be at LEGO.com in using it on the site.

After talking to a couple of people, I worked my way to a Project Manager in charge of games who was interested in reviewing the piece. The response was excellent, and I was told that our solution would be passed up the ranks to her bosses, who would not have an opportunity to see it for a couple of weeks because they were in Denmark.

There were a few conversations about the piece, and we left the opportunity open to discuss moving forward together as soon as an opportunity presented itself. Regardless of what happens next, the project was a success. Not only were we able to sharpen our Flash 5 skills, but we now had an open door with LEGO for the right opportunity. Mission accomplished!

Post-Mortem

When all was done, this was a great project to explore and one I feel could still be considered a success. We have showcased it to other potential clients, and it proved to help win the accounts. I also think that next time we are at LEGO, we could use this to prove our capabilities along with the rest of our portfolio. The important lesson here is that we cannot wait for opportunities to come to us all the time; sometimes we have to go to them.

Should we find more time to work on this, I would like to enable the picture feature that would produce a GIF of the workspace and automatically e-mail it to LEGO via a form. LEGO could then hold contests and post the most interesting creations on the site.

To be consumer-ready, we also would have to improve the grid snapping to be more precise and come up with an intelligent way to handle layering. My thinking is to provide the users with a grouping tool so they could grab groups of blocks on the workspace and delete or move them. Another interesting concept would be to enable individual block deleting from the workspace. The user could identify a block on the workspace with a pointing tool, highlight it, and delete it without having to drag it. Maybe we could even enable gravity so that other blocks fall into shape? Endless possibilities, particularly if you look at all the cool new building sets LEGO has.

CHAPTER 6

Furniture.com's Room Planner

PROFESSIONAL

The innovative Flash Room Planner.

Overview

You might not have heard of Intellisync, or Pumatech, or even my company, Hookumu, Inc. Although you probably haven't heard of Design Mentor, you will in the coming years. In the Flash community, most veterans have heard of Furniture.com's Room Planner.

When the Room Planner was launched, the company where I was working at the time, Internoded Incorporated, received about three inquiries a week from prospective clients to other Flash developers about how we built it. We even had people e-mailing us with offers to lease or purchase the solution.

I saved this chapter for last because I wanted to make sure that my writing skills were at their best before working on this case study. Little did I know that a rare marketing opportunity, with a deadline, would present itself and force me to write this chapter in four short days.

It's interesting to me that I am actually writing about the Room Planner. Just two years ago, the very idea of writing a book about the Room Planner that included its source code would have been unthinkable. After all, it was our claim to fame at the time; no one else had even approached what we had done, and in some cases, still have not. We wouldn't have considered giving away the source code for the price of a book. It's amazing how much has changed since then...

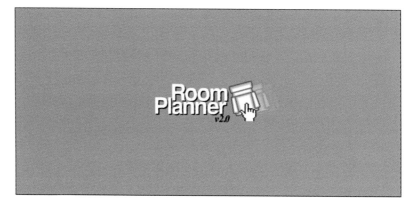

Figure 6.1   *Finally, a picture of the Room Planner!*

The Players

It was November 1999, and I was working for a company in Cambridge, MA called Internoded Incorporated. We were a small but strong team of developers and designers, offering exceptional custom Internet solutions for some pretty large clientele. My job was primarily to handle the interface and Web designs of the many projects we had going. I had a small team of creatives and technologists working for me, and when we weren't working on the larger initiatives, I dabbled in Flash, creating product demos and animations.

At the time, we were a part of the Beta team testing Flash 4 before it had been released. Many people knew about Flash at the time, but it was version 3 and basically had no scripting control, and only limited interactivity. We got to work with Macromedia because ours was one of the only consulting shops that was using Flash for something more than simple animations. We were primarily using Flash to create business applications and product demos.

We saw a market opportunity and tried to leverage it, but it was microcosmic in size compared to the projects we had been working on. Needless to say, it was far more interesting work to me than HTML, GIFs, and JavaScript, and in an effort to solicit more of this type of work from companies other than our current clients, I purchased a spot on Macromedia's Developer Listing.

Figure 6.2   *Can I get some light over here, please? The Furniture.com logo.*

It was only a few weeks later that I received the call from Furniture.com. It goes without saying that I was very excited about the possibilities, although I knew nothing about what they wanted other than they were looking for an advanced Flash solution, and found our name on Macromedia's Developer Listing. (That should be reason enough for you all to go get listed with Macromedia right now.)

Unsure of the group to take along, I decided to keep the visiting team small and capable. Attending on Internoded's behalf would be our Sales Manager Spike Fry and myself. Spike and I had a great deal of success selling as a team, being able to play off each other and adapt to the situation as necessary.

So, Spike and I visited Furniture.com in their still unfinished space in Framingham, MA. As I mentioned in Chapter 2, "George the Cat Holiday Card," the space was unbelievable; however, at this point in the story, it was completely under construction. We entered the large, typical corporate building to a common lobby where a sign pointed us to the top, second floor that was all Furniture.com. Odd, I thought, as the building was quite large for it all to be Furniture.com's. Odder yet was that as we approached the top of the stairs, we were greeted by the scene of the front of a house. Although we were inside, the entrance to the office was renovated to look like the exterior of a house, complete with high-end front oak door with etched glass, a doorknocker, plants, exterior lights on both sides— remember, we were inside!

We entered the space to an even greater surprise: The entire interior of the space had been built to look like a house. There were six conference rooms filled with high-end dining room furniture, complete with paintings on the walls and armoires, but that wasn't even the most surprising part. The entire middle of the whole floor was the house that we came into. Around the outside the house—but still in the building—was the exterior of the house, complete with vinyl siding and a section of roof that ran around the entire space. There was an interior kitchen with a full patio, complete with picnic tables and patio furniture. There was a regulation basketball hoop above a functioning garage door, behind which the IT guys built the computers. The list goes on and on. It was amazing what VC money could buy you. I do have to say it was then, and still is, by far the coolest working environment I have ever seen.

Spike and I were sitting in the lobby (a living room) when Misha Katz came to greet us. Misha was co-founder of Furniture.com and, at 21, was wise beyond his years. Misha deserves the most credit for the Room Planner as its original conceiver. With Misha was Steve Guttfriend, a.k.a. Yechezchal, a.k.a. Gutty who would eventually be the first to write the ActionScript for the Room Planner.

So, the four of us sat in an unfinished, house-like office space, in a conference room with no table and four chairs we had to wheel in from other rooms. We started the conversation with Internoded's capabilities and quickly gravitated to Furniture.com's needs.

The Client's Need: Increased Conversion Rates

At the time, Furniture.com was about two years old, having started as a traditional brick-and-mortar furniture retailer. About a year prior to our meeting, Misha and the other co-founder, Steve Rothchild, had posted a bulletin board system and a simple Web site that gave only product information and prices. You still had to call to place an order. To their surprise, and mine, people were buying the furniture. A business was born.

Over the past twelve months, the company had been building an online catalog of furniture. At the time of our meeting, the company had about 120 employees and an active e-commerce Web site that allowed customers to view furniture, order swatches of fabric that would arrive at their houses within two days, and save a wish list of items. The company had even spent a great deal of money procuring the Furniture.com domain name. It was clearly making strides to become the dominant online furnishing retailer.

Our first question, of course, was whether people would actually spend thousands of dollars on a couch or mahogany table without being able to touch it first. Apparently, the answer to that question was yes, but not without a number of supportive programs and site features. Potential customers had many reassuring programs that enabled them to make the leap from browser to buyer including an excellent product line, free delivery, money-back guarantee, 24-hour customer support, and an arsenal of information about the product they were interested in.

In fact, it was determined that many people had enough faith to purchase furniture online without ever having seen it. At its peak, Furniture.com had revenues of millions of dollars per month. We also discovered that the more information you could give the potential customer, the more likely that customer was to become a buyer. We called the process of making browsers into buyers *conversion*. The higher the conversion rate, the better the site and the company were doing their jobs.

This is why Misha had us in for a meeting. He had an idea of how to increase conversion rates by developing a tool that could do something not even the traditional furniture stores could do yet. So, Misha explained the basic concept of the Room Planner on a rolled-up sketch of the interface he had with him.

In this initial two-hour meeting, we explored potential features and functionality as well as timelines and cost. Everything seemed doable, but there were some really unknown concerns. In fact, Flash 4 had been released only one week before this meeting. This was great because Flash finally provided the drag-and-drop functionality crucial to the Room Planner's success. Flash also now had the ability to talk with external data sources such as ASP pages and databases.

Another concern was that much of the requested functionality required Macromedia's Generator product, which was still in version 1 and wouldn't be compatible with Flash version 4.0 for several months. It was when this came up in the meeting that Misha mentioned that Furniture.com wanted this solution in the next three weeks!

Figure 6.3   *I thought you bought generators at Sears?*

After refraining from laughing, gasping, and appearing stunned, I told Misha that this was possible, but because of the untested technology, we might encounter many unknown roadblocks. In fact, I told him that there was the possibility that we would encounter a technical issue that could take us weeks to figure out and might compromise the deadline. Later, I learned this was the very reason we won the account. Apparently there wasn't much competition at the time for this type of work, and those who did have conversations about the Room Planner with Misha raised no issues or concerns, which in itself was a major concern. I have learned over the years that the best approach with any client is to be direct and upfront about the entire project from the beginning. If your services and pricing are solid, good clients will embrace this honesty and you will have a better chance of winning the account. Clients who do not understand the issues involved in building leading-edge solutions are typically not the types of clients you want in the long run anyway.

The Solution

Before I get on to explaining the solution and how we went about building it, I would first like to strongly suggest that you take a look at the Room Planner Tour file included on the CD-ROM. The Tour is a Flash demo of the Room Planner that lets you see it in action and describes its functionality.

The demo's original purpose was to educate Furniture.com browsers on how to use the Room Planner before they jumped in.

The Room Planner itself is just a small Flash file that pulls all its information from the Furniture.com databases, ASP pages, and additional SWFs. Without this data, it isn't possible to get it working. Now that Furniture.com has ceased operations, the databases have been shut down and you can't see the Room Planner in action. The Tour does a great job of re-creating the action in the Room Planner.

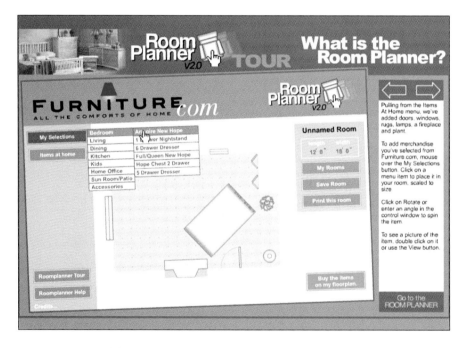

Figure 6.4   *"Today, I'll be your guide as we tour the lovely Room Planner."*

Before I dive into the Flash file, let me preface all this with a few comments. First, everyone should know that the Room Planner was built in Flash 4 and never had the opportunity to be rebuilt in Flash 5. I've commented about

Flash 4 versus Flash 5 ActionScripting syntax in the first five chapters, and I hope you get the idea by now. For the Room Planner case study, I would rather focus on how we pushed Flash beyond its capabilities at the time; for example, by not using Generator and making Flash handle all the content. I think a lot can be learned from that.

I'd also like to mention the fact that we are currently developing a similar, yet far more advanced, solution for a high-profile client. If all goes well with this book, I hope to share everything we have learned on that project with you, whether in a second edition of this book or on the Hookumu site. So, if you can be patient until early 2002, I will discuss how to create the next generation Room Planner in Flash 5 with Macromedia Generator.

You should also know that there simply is not enough room to discuss every function and line of code in the Room Planner, and I feel this is beyond the scope of the book. The Room Planner has approximately 1000 lines of ActionScripting spread out among 15 movie clips. There are also 500 lines of code spread out among 60 buttons, and 75 icons with three lines of code each. It also has 30 ASP pages communicating with a 20,000-product catalog residing in a SQL Server database. Because I doubt you bought this book to learn all about ASP and SQL databases, I have instead chosen to cover the overall architecture of the Room Planner so that you get a complete picture, highlight the most innovative and interesting features, and explore how the functionality works.

Overall Architecture

There are essentially three technical components to the Room Planner. A SQL database contains all the Furniture.com product information. We also stored all the users' information, such as access information, saved rooms, location, position of icons on the floor, and more. I will not cover the details of the database other than noting that the information in this database changed almost every minute. Whether it was the addition or removal of products or users changing their info, the Room Planner had to be able to handle dynamic information.

The second component to the Room Planner is the ASP pages. Essentially, the ASP pages allow the database and the Room Planner SWF to talk to one another. We will be taking some peeks into these pages at a basic level.

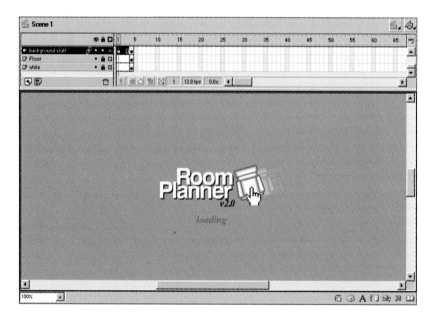

Figure 6.5 *Just four frames?!*

The central component to the Room Planner is the main Flash file itself, which is one scene with four frames. The first three frames are for pre-loading. This is the ultimate in efficient Flash design and scripting because all the action originates from one frame in Flash.

Let's first look at this file from the approach of a first-time user with no saved rooms or last rooms to load automatically. I'll get into how that works in the details. The Flash file itself is divided into five basic parts: initializing and setup; the help screen and tour; the icon/floor interface; room functions; and buying the items. I will briefly describe each of these components so that you get the big picture and then drill down into more detail. Stay with me now!

Initializing and Setup

First is the initialization of the Room Planner itself. I will skip over the pre-loader because I have talked about these enough in this book and this one is not particularly unique. Feel free to explore the code for this in the Flash file at your leisure.

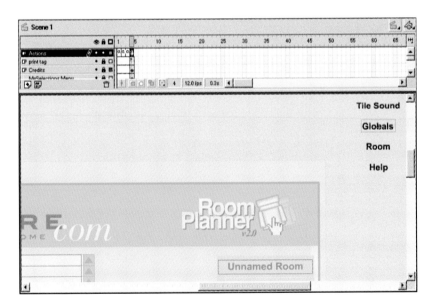

Figure 6.6   *What's* GLOBALS *doing way over there?*

When the SWF is done loading, it calls to a Movie Clip— placed off the stage in the Actions layer—with the instance name of GLOBALS and tells it to get going. GLOBALS calls to an ASP page called fetchGlobals.asp, which sets up all the basic parameters including the scale, the default room name, the size, and so on.

GLOBALS also tells a Movie Clip named ROOM to initialize. ROOM, located just under GLOBALS on the Actions layer, uses the default room sizes and name to tell the floor what size to be and what the room name should be. We also tell the FLOOR Movie Clip to initialize, which sizes itself to the defaults.

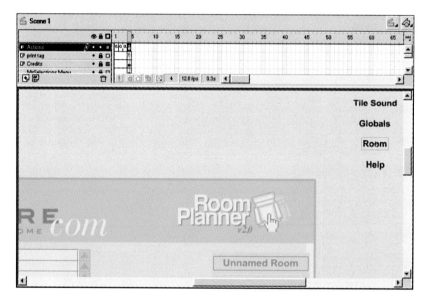

Figure 6.7 *Looks like* GLOBALS *and* ROOM *are hanging out.*

We then pull in whatever selections the user has made while shopping on the Furniture.com site. Let me explain. If you look at the tour or the source file, you will see two icons in the upper-left corner of the Room Planner workspace. The first is called My Selections, and contains a set of dynamically loaded icons that match exactly those items that the user has added to his shopping cart, or wish list, while browsing the site. These are the products the user intends to eventually purchase. Approximately sixty icons make up the other set, called Items at Home. These represent most any item you could have in your house. This obviously includes most every type of furniture, but also architectural items such as fireplaces, windows, doors, and at one point, even a dog that you could have lying around.

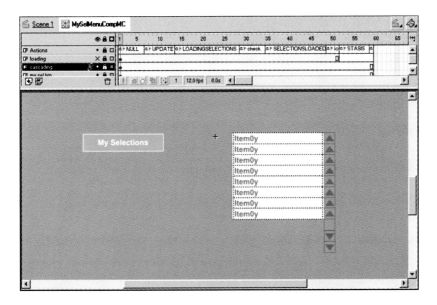

Figure 6.8   *M-m-my selections.*

There are three major differentiators between the two types of icons. The simplest is color. We wanted users to be able to easily differentiate those items on their desktop that represented items that already existed in their homes and those that represented actual Furniture.com products. Another differentiator is that the Items at Home had no pictures associated with them. For Furniture.com icons, there is an active link that the user could click to see actual product information for that item launched into a new browser window. The final and biggest differentiator is the ability to represent the actual Furniture.com items to scale. That is, all Furniture.com products had actual width and depth measurements associated with them that needed to be fixed, unaltered, and represented to scale on the floor. One of the greatest uses of the Room Planner is the ability for users to do somewhat accurate space planning to determine whether the new furniture they purchased would fit within their space. Because of this, we also needed to give users the ability to scale those icons that represented the items in their home.

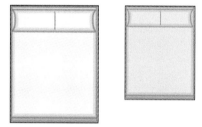

Figure 6.9   *One of these icons is not like the other.*

We load the icons from the user's shopping cart by pulling the information from the site with the fetchSelections.asp file. This page brings in the items that are in the user's shopping cart by name and ID number. If this were a returning user, we would also pull in all the saved room names from fetchRooms.asp and set up the last room the user was working on as the active floor with the furniture in the last position the user left it. It was very cool seeing this happen for the first time.

I will get into all this in more detail in a minute. I'll stay at a high level and cover the remaining four major pieces to the Room Planner first.

Help Screen and Tour

The next simple pieces to cover are the Help files and the Tour. The Help information is simply an external SWF that is loaded from the following script when the user clicks the Help button:

```
on (release) {
    duplicateMovieClip ("/HELP0", "HELP", 200);
    loadMovie ("help.swf", "/HELP");
    setProperty ("/HELP", _x, 146);
    setProperty ("/HELP", _y, 12);
}
```

This script duplicates a Movie Clip on the main timeline called HELP0, loads the external help.SWF file, and repositions it on the stage so that it appears in the correct place. What is displayed to the user is just a series of sentences that describe the basic Room Planner features and how the user works with them.

The Tour is another SWF file that is launched in an external browser window. External SWF loads help to keep initial downloads to a minimum. The Tour, as you've most likely seen by now, is an animated demonstration of the Room Planner in action. This went a great distance in helping new users work with the Room Planner.

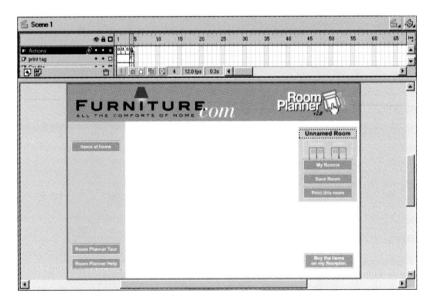

Figure 6.10   *The workspace just before exporting.*

Icon and Floor Interface

The next component to cover is the interface, which is made up of the floor and the actual icons themselves. The floor is a significant element that starts at a scale of 20×17 feet. It can be resized up to 40×34 feet in scale. If the user enters a number in either field that is larger than 20 or 17, the room will automatically resize to the larger scale. Inversely, if the user has a large floor—greater than 20×17—and enters a number that is below the 20×17 scale, the floor and all room elements will scale to the smaller scale. When these transitions happen, all of the icons are unloaded, the `scale` is reset, and the icons are reloaded using the new scale ratio.

Interestingly enough, this feature was added at a later date. Initially, we had only the 20×17 room size thinking that this would be sufficient, only to learn later that people were complaining they had bathrooms larger than this!

Figure 6.11 *Make that floor bigger!*

There is one minor issue with this solution. If a user is in the larger scale, places items outside of the room, and then shrinks the room, those items will be unreachable unless the user goes back to the larger scale. The items are still there, but they are beyond the visible workspace. We also needed to accommodate odd-shaped rooms. The plan was to implement a series of odd-shaped floors that users could start with and then dynamically drag into the correct shape of their room, but we never did get to it before the decline of the company. What we did create is a series of basic floor–colored positive and negative shapes. These shapes could be placed on the floor to create the desired room layout.

As for the furniture, any time the user creates an icon from her selections or from the generic items, we duplicate an empty movie—which is located off the workspace—on to the floor. The empty Movie Clip is called the TILE, and it is 100×100 pixels in size. We load the incoming icon of the furniture piece the user wants to place on his floor plan into the TILE. Because we know the ID number of the furniture the user selected, we can look to the database via an ASP page and determine the size of the furniture so that we can scale the icon appropriately.

Figure 6.12 *Where all the furniture is born.*

As mentioned before, generic furniture items that are already in the user's home can be scaled and rotated as necessary. However, the Furniture.com furniture can only be rotated. We can't have users planning a room by changing the actual dimensions of the furniture they would be buying. Both resizing and rotating of the icons are accomplished easily by changing their attributes in a small pop-up control panel that appears over each icon.

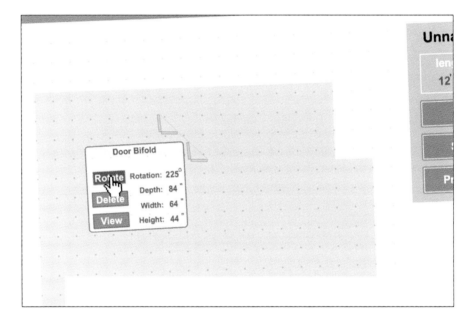

Figure 6.13   *I need control!*

Room Functions

Room functions, such as the ability to save, create new rooms, and delete rooms, all work basically the same way. Each registered user has a set of files in the database with all his data in them. When the user saves a room, we call saveRoom.asp and update the room information in the database. When the user renames the room, see Figure 6.14, we call renameRoom.asp, and so on. I will cover the ASP pages in more detail later.

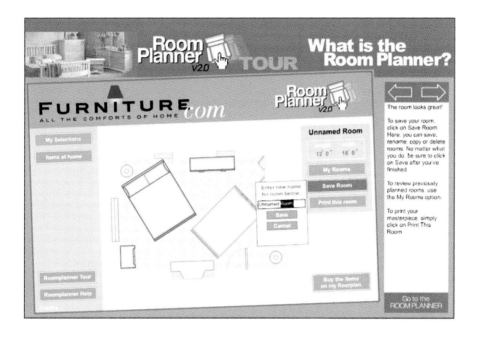

Figure 6.14   *What should I call this room? Joey, Spot? Doug?*

If the user decides to start a new room or delete the current room, we must clear what she currently has in the workspace. If the user loads a room, we clear the current room and bring in all the data needed to re-create all the items and resize the floor accordingly. The printing room function would take care of itself with the Flash 5 plug-in. However, when we started, that was not the case. The early Flash 4 plug-in did not print and this was a major drawback. Users surely wanted the ability to print a copy of the floor layout they created. At one point, we used the developers edition of Generator to create a GIF of the screen, and embedded it in an ASP page that the user could print.

As we were working out the bugs, and had in fact released it to the live solution, Macromedia updated the

Flash plug-in to handle printing, so we pulled out the Generator components. This allowed the solution to perform faster and required less maintenance and concern on our end. Generator was new to everyone and it concerned us. This is a good example of constantly making sure that you are aware of the latest plug-ins and technologies available to provide your clients with the best possible solution.

Buying the Furniture

Finally, the user has the ability to purchase just those items that are on his workspace. When the user decides he likes the layout and will buy the items in the current room, he clicks the Buy button at the bottom right of the screen. (See Figure 6.15.) This button calls to saveRoom.asp to make sure that the room is saved, and then just gathers the product information on the floor with ID numbers and passes this to an ASP page named purchase.asp. This file passes the data into the current Furniture.com e-commerce system and the user simply finishes the checkout process he normally would. This component was very cool because it assumed that the user wanted to purchase only the items on the floor and not those in his entire wish list.

Okay, are you still with me? Hopefully, at this point, you understand the overall features of the Room Planner and the three types of technology used: Flash, ASP, and SQL. In addition, you should have a basic understanding of the five components that make up the Flash file and an idea of the amount of code involved. Now let's really dive in and get our hands dirty.

Basic Layout and Construction

First, I would like you to understand the basic layout of the file and why things are constructed as they are. There are essentially five layers to keep in mind. Technically there are more, but this is for organizational purposes.

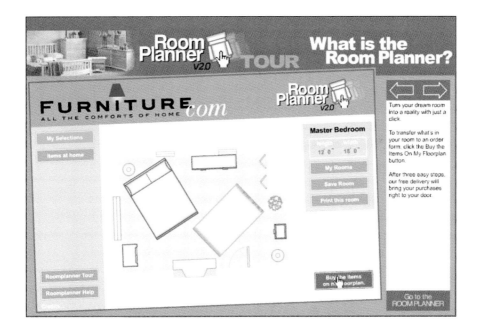

Figure 6.15 *Cha-ching!*

The lowest functional layer is called Floor. The Floor itself is a Movie Clip that contains all the tiles and control panel components. This includes the TILE Movie Clip (also called decal) into which each of the furniture icons will be loaded. Remember the tile is the generic 100×100 shape that we load all the icons into before scaling. Tile is a Movie Clip located within the Floor Movie Clip on the main timeline. Also in the Floor Movie Clip is the control panel Movie Clip that contains all the controls to allow the user to scale, rotate, view, and delete icons. Having the Floor MC on the lowest layer and self-contained ensures that none of these items appears on top of menus or other interface elements.

Above the floor is a layer titled background stuff, which is for design elements of the Room Planner. This includes screen components that are not menus or buttons, such as navigation designs and the logo.

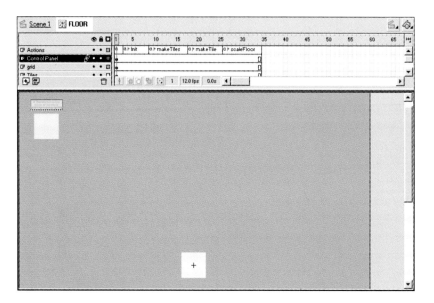

Figure 6.16 *The* Floor *Movie Clip with the* TILE *and* decal *tucked away in the upper corner.*

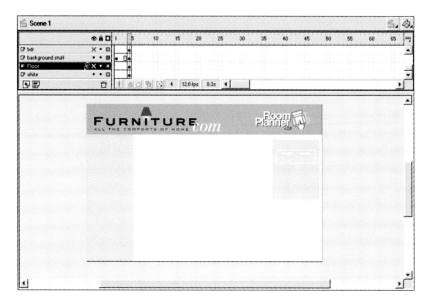

Figure 6.17 *Just the graphics please.*

Above the background stuff layer are several layers for the
menus and buttons. All the menus and buttons needed to
be stacked carefully so that there would never be overlaps
or things hidden underneath another item. As you can
imagine, this took several revisions before the correct
combination was determined.

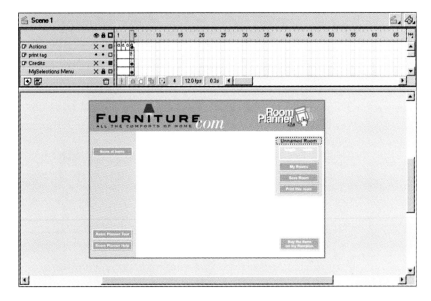

Figure 6.18   *Nice buttons.*

On the top layer are a few components that always needed
to be over everything else, such as the credits that appear
when the user clicks the Credits button. This was done for
two reasons. First, Macromedia allows anyone to develop
and distribute Flash solutions that can be viewed with the
free plug-in as long as the Made With Macromedia logo is in
the solution. We decided the credits screen would be a
good place for this, and we also wanted to include
Internoded credits for obvious business development
reasons.

Finally, there is an Actions layer that holds what we will call the *controller* movies. It doesn't matter where this layer is in the stack because there is nothing visual in the movies. The two main controller movies are GLOBALS and ROOM, both located off stage. The Movie Clip that contains all the sounds, called TileSound, is also on this layer. By having all the sounds in one place, we could easily adjust or change the sounds without having to go into every button and Movie Clip throughout the piece, as discussed in earlier chapters.

Basic Scripting

Now that you get the idea about the layering that is going on, let's discuss the scripting. Almost all the functioning code is in one of four places: GLOBALS, FLOOR, ROOM, or TILE. Having said that, there is plenty going on inside each menu and button. Let's first run through what happens at launch and then start looking at some scripts. Of course, we have a loading screen, and then we arrive at the fourth frame I keep talking about where everything starts to happen.

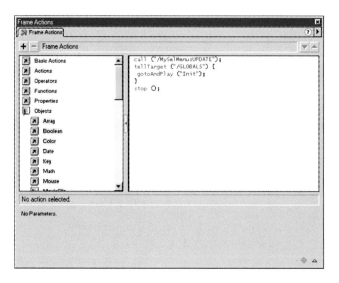

Figure 6.19　*The fourth frame is where everything starts.*

```
call ("/MySelMenu:UPDATE");
tellTarget ("/GLOBALS") {
   gotoAndPlay ("Init");
}
stop ();
```

That's it? All this talk and only five lines of code? Yup, now let's show you why. The `call` function simply calls out to an ASP page to update the items in the users My Selections list (I'll cover this more in detail in a minute.) We then tell the Movie Clip GLOBALS that is located off of the visible stage to go to and play the frame labeled Init, where it encounters the following script:

```
DONE = false;
call ("fetchGlobals");
resume = "Start";
gotoAndPlay ("WaitForDone");
```

Most of the script here is straightforward. The variable DONE is set to false and we call out to the frame labeled fetchGlobals. We'll take a look at this in a moment. You will often see the variable resume set to Start throughout the code. Start is the frame label that the loop will go to when it is finished looping. This ensures that it continues to loop.

The last line sends the user to the frame in GLOBALS labeled WaitForDone, which initializes a simple loop that continues until the data being pulled in on the fetchGlobals frame sets the DONE variable to true. We will see resume and DONE again, but I'll assume that you understand it to keep from being repetitive.

The most important function here is the call from the GLOBALS Movie Clip to the fetchGlobals frame, which contains only the following code:

```
loadVariables ("fetchGlobals.asp", "/GLOBALS");
```

This tells the Room Planner to go get the `fetchGlobals` ASP pages. These pages contain data from the database and dump their variables into the Movie Clip GLOBALS. The returned results look like this:

```
UserID=1234 & Registered=yes & DefaultInchToPix=2 &
➡DefaultPixToInch=1/2 & DefaultRoomName="Unnamed Room" &
➡DefaultUserID=384 & DefaultRoomWidth=20*12 &
➡DefaultRoomDepth=17*12 & MinTileWidth=2 &
➡MinTileDepth=2 & MaxTileWidth=20*12 &
➡MaxTileDepth=17*12 & MaxRooms=30 & MaxTiles=27 & DONE=1
```

In this string of data are key elements that will be used throughout the piece. `UserID` identifies whose information we should be collecting to and from the database. `Registered` tells us whether we need to send the user to a registration screen on the site before we allow the user to purchase or save room information. Users don't have to be registered, but we can't save their data for later or let them proceed to purchase without getting more information.

When the user registers, her ID is saved in a cookie that the Room Planner accesses via an ASP page. The ASP page contains URL strings and VBScript to pass information from the Room Planner to the database and vice versa.

Another very important indicator is the scale ratio, which is called `DefaultInchToPix` and is currently set to 2 in this example. This ratio means that every two pixels onscreen equals one inch in reality. We use this to scale the floor and every furniture icon. All the ASP calls, meaning the communication between the Room Planner and the database, work the same way regardless of which way the information is traveling.

Furniture Icons

Initially, we wanted to have a spectrum of icons that would cover anything the user would want to put in a room. We started with a running list of icons that we thought would be necessary. After we felt the list was complete, we had about 100 icons and we needed a way to validate that nothing was missing. So, we had one of the people responsible for tracking all of the information on the Furniture.com Web site supply us with a spreadsheet of the types of items that users had in their carts, as shown in Figure 6.20. This information was invaluable because it confirmed what users were buying and ensured that we had an icon for each.

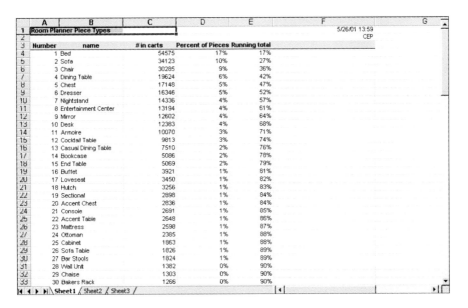

Figure 6.20   *What icons do we need?*

A team of designers including Phil, a designer and Creative Director from Furniture.com, and myself set a series of guidelines around the design of each icon and we went down the list, creating the icons one by one until we had approximately 100.

One of the more interesting parts of the Room Planner is how we handled the furniture icons. Each icon is a SWF loaded from outside of the Room Planner when that icon is needed. We did it this way so that the Room Planner itself would be small, download quickly, and load only what it needed. After all, our research clearly indicated that the targeted audience for the Room Planner was at large stay-at-home moms using AOL. This evolved as e-commerce became more popular, but we wanted to focus on the less technical buyer in our customer pool and this seemed accurate. Loading one small icon at a time, as needed, is far more efficient and unnoticeable than pre-loading everything whether or not the user wants it.

One of the biggest issues we encountered was sizing the icons appropriately. For example, we had one sofa icon that had to represent anything from a small kids' sofa up to a huge queen sleeper sofa. Flash scales things based on numeric values, not inches. We knew that all the data coming in for the items would be in inches, so we created a 100×100 pixel–Movie Clip that would contain each of the icons. Although Flash is a vector program, it still thinks in pixels. We had to have a means of converting the inch dimensions of the furniture into pixels for accurate sizing and display in the screen. By placing and stretching the icon in the 100×100 pixel tile, we could use the pixel-to-inch ratio from the `fetchGlobals.asp` file to scale only the tile and the furniture icon would scale accurately.

This presented a small design problem if the user took a relatively square icon, such as an ottoman, and stretched it disproportionately. For example, at 2 feet by 10 feet, the line widths would scale as well and there would be heavy lines on the stretched sides and thin lines on the squashed sides. To alleviate this as much as possible, we ensured that line weights were minimal and equal on every side.

Figure 6.21   *Holy ottoman, Batman!*

By bringing all the icons into one empty Movie Clip, called TILE with the load movie command, we also accomplished some other things. In TILE, we have named frames that control the different actions and functions we need for each icon.

There is an invisible button inside the TILE Movie Clip, which is inside the FLOOR Movie Clip. Placing them inside of FLOOR ensures that when they are duplicated (loaded), they don't end up above the menus and other elements. This button has the following code associated with it:

```
on (release, releaseOutside) {
    call ("../:release");
}
on (rollOver) {
    call ("../:over");
}
on (rollOut) {
    call ("../:out");
}
on (press) {
    call ("../:press");
}
```

When the user releases the button, Flash moves to the release frame in the TILE Movie Clip, where the following script is encountered:

Listing 6.1   Frame Script at Release

```
1: tellTarget ("decal") {
2:     prevFrame ();
3: }
4: myX = int(getProperty("", _x)/(/ROOM:InchToPix));
5: myY = int(getProperty("", _y)/(/ROOM:InchToPix));
6: set ("/ROOM:tile" add ID add "_x", myX);
7: set ("/ROOM:tile" add ID add "_y", myY);
8: oldTime = newTime;
9: newTime = getTimer();
10: if ((Number((newTime-oldTime))<500) and ours) {
11:     getURL ("viewPicture.asp", "_blank", "POST");
12: }
13: call ("/FLOOR/CP:come");
14: stopDrag ();
```

Line 1 tells the icon to go to the static state, meaning the normal state indicating that icon is not active. Lines 4 and 5 determine the exact location of where the icon is on the desktop.

Lines 6 and 7 update the data in the ROOM Movie Clip so that the tile actually does move to the correct location. Lines 8 and 9 are creating the double-click simulation. In Flash, there is no standard way to determine whether the user double-clicks on something, only a single click. In the code, we set two variables upon release of the button. If the two variables, oldTime and newTime, are less than 500 milliseconds apart, Flash knows that the user is double-clicking and the control panel launches the new window to view the picture of the furniture in it.

Line 13 tells the control panel to launch or show itself. Just to remind you, the control panel is the small panel that appears next to each icon when the user clicks it; the control panel allows for scaling, rotating, item renaming, and so on. Line 14 tells the dragging to stop.

However, if the user is just rolling over the button in the TILE MC, the code in Listing 6.2, located in the over frame, goes into action.

Listing 6.2   Frame Script on the over **Frame**

```
1: setProperty ("/FLOOR/CPOff", _visible, true);
2: /FLOOR/CP:tileNum = ID;
3: tellTarget ("decal") {
4:     nextFrame ();
5: }
6: tellTarget ("/TileSound") {
7:     gotoAndStop ("click");
8: }
9: call ("/FLOOR/CP:come");
```

Line 1 turns on the control panel Rolloff button. This is an invisible button larger than the control panel itself that hides the control panel when the user rolls off the control panel and onto the invisible Rolloff button. Sounds confusing, but if you look at the source file it's pretty straightforward.

Line 2 tells the control panel which tile (furniture icon) we are dealing with. Line 3 tells the icon to go into the rollover state and line 6 tells the sound effect to play. Line 9 tells the control panel to show itself.

Out is the frame that Flash goes to when the user rolls off the button. When this occurs, the following code executes and resets the icon to the normal state:

```
tellTarget ("decal") {
    prevFrame ();
}
```

Finally, we have the press frame, which executes when the user clicks and holds:

```
setProperty ("/FLOOR/CP", _visible, false);
tellTarget ("decal") {
        nextFrame ();
}
tellTarget ("/TileSound") {
        gotoAndStop ("drag");
}
startDrag ("", false, -245, -210, 245, 210);
```

Line 1 tells the control panel to go away, because we assume that the user is initiating a drag. Line 2 tells the icon to go into the drag state, which is just a color change. Line 5 plays the drag sound, and line 8 sets the parameters for how far the icon can be dragged.

As you can see, each basic button function, such as rollover, press, and so on, is sent to a different frame in the TILE Movie Clip. This makes editing the functions much easier. The following is the code in the TILE movie clip frames to which the button refers, but first a note: Each icon has three states to it representing static, over, and active. In the following frames, you'll see tellTarget commands to those frames.

```
ours = false;
DecalDone = false;
newTime = getTimer();
stop ();
```

This code, from the frame labeled Init in the TILE Movie Clip, just defines some variables that we will use later on. The ours variable is used to determine whether the icon is for a generic icon—meaning an item of furniture the user already has in her home—or a Furntiture.com item for which we need to control the height and width. The DecalDone variable is just to make sure that the icon is fully loaded before we do anything with it, and the NewTime variable is used for the double-clicking trick explained earlier. The next line is from the frame labeled `generic`, which is the start of the creation sequence for a generic icon:

```
play ();
```

This next line is for the frame labeled `check1` and is part of the loop for a generic icon that will loop until the icon arrives. We do this by placing a frame action setting the variable of `DecalDone` to true in the last frame of each icon.

243

```
if (not DecalDone) {
    gotoAndPlay ("generic");
} else {
    call ("decalSet");
    tellTarget ("decal") {
        gotoAndStop (1);
    }
    gotoAndPlay ("scale");
}
```

The following code for the frame labeled `decalSet` just sets the position of the incoming icon. `setProperty` sets the x and y positions using the variables `decalX` and `decalY`, respectively.

```
setProperty ("decal", _x, getProperty("decal", _x)-
➥decalX);
setProperty ("decal", _y, getProperty("decal", _y)-
➥decalY);
setProperty ("decal", _alpha, 75);
```

This next set of script is for the frame labeled `scale`:

```
decalWidth = eval("/ROOM:tile" add ID add
➥"_decalWidth");
decalDepth = eval("/ROOM:tile" add ID add
➥"_decalDepth");
scaleW = newWidth/decalWidth;
scaleD = newDepth/decalDepth;
setProperty ("", _xscale, scaleW*100);
setProperty ("", _yscale, scaleD*100);
stop ();
```

This code scales the icon to the correct size with the setProperty functions. If the icon is a Furniture.com item, it does basically the same thing in the frame labeled ours with a simple play function and pulls the actual furniture sizes from the fetchOurs.asp that pulls the data from the database.

In the frame labeled check2, we encounter the following code:

```
if (not DecalDone) {
    gotoAndPlay ("ours");
}
```

This essentially loops back to the frame labeled ours and keeps checking to see whether the icon has arrived yet.

The next bit of code is for the frame labeled checkOurs:

```
ours = true;
call ("decalSet");
tellTarget ("decal") {
    gotoAndStop (4);
}
fetchPFID = eval("/ROOM:tile" add ID add "_pfID");
```

Again we call to the decalSet frame to position the icon. Normally, in the movie clip, this is the order so that after the Furniture.com item is positioned, it goes right into the scale frame. The next frames just handle what happens when the icon is dealt with. This is found in the frame labeled over:

```
setProperty ("/FLOOR/CPOff", _visible, true);
```

This code turns on the control panel Roll Off button. We needed a safe way to have the control panel stay open when the user was over it, but also a way to have it go away when the user was done. Inside the FLOOR Movie Clip, we put a huge button that, when rolled over, tells the control panel to go away. This line of code just makes the control panel visible. When the button is rolled over, the control panel becomes invisible again.

```
/FLOOR/CP:tileNum = ID;
```

This is just passing the variable of which tile we're dealing with to the control panel.

```
tellTarget ("decal") {
    nextFrame ();
}
```

This sets the icon's state to rollover.

```
tellTarget ("/TileSound") {
    gotoAndStop ("click");
}
```

This tells the sound movie clip which sound to play.

```
call ("/FLOOR/CP:come");
```

This tells the control panel to show itself—I will cover this in greater detail in a moment. The next bit of code is from the frame labeled press:

```
press
setProperty ("/FLOOR/CP", _visible, false);
turn off the CP
tellTarget ("decal") {
    nextFrame ();
}
```

This tells the icon to go to the drag state.

```
tellTarget ("/TileSound") {
    gotoAndStop ("drag");
}
startDrag ("", false, -245, -210, 245, 210);
```

From the frame labeled release:

```
tellTarget ("decal") {
    prevFrame ();
}
```

This tells the icon to go to the static state.

```
myX = int(getProperty("", _x)/(/ROOM:InchToPix));
myY = int(getProperty("", _y)/(/ROOM:InchToPix));
```

This determines where the icon is currently positioned on the screen.

```
set ("/ROOM:tile" add ID add "_x", myX);
set ("/ROOM:tile" add ID add "_y", myY);
```

This updates the data in the ROOM Movie Clip.

```
oldTime = newTime;
newTime = getTimer();
if ((Number((newTime-oldTime))<500) and ours) {
    getURL ("viewPicture.asp", "_blank", "POST");
}
```

These few lines create the double-click trick, as above. It then launches the view window, but only if it's a Furniture.com item, of course, because the generic icons have no pictures associated with them.

```
call ("/FLOOR/CP:come");
stopDrag ();
```

We then close out the code and stop the drag. The next group of scripting is found in the frame labeled out:

```
tellTarget ("decal") {
    prevFrame ();
}
```

This is used from the control panel. When someone uses the scaling function in the control panel, it is updated here.

```
newWidth = newWidth*((/ROOM:InchToPix)/2);
newDepth = newDepth*((/ROOM:InchToPix)/2);
gotoAndStop ("scale");
```

Control Panel

Now, let's talk in more detail about the functionality enabled by the control panel. We need to outfit each icon with drag-and-drop functionality and that's simple enough. But we also need to deal with additional functionality such as rotation, scaling, and deletion. In addition, Furniture.com items need to link to pictures of the products.

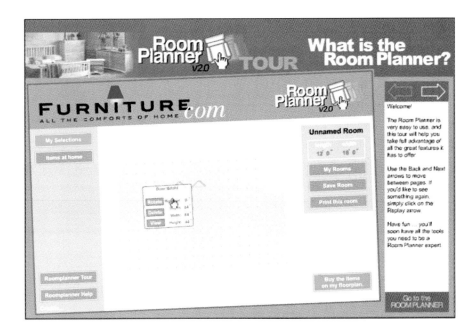

Figure 6.22   *Who's in control here?*

There were many ways we could have implemented this and decided on using the control panel approach you see in the tour. This did present many issues, though, such as identifying when the control panel would appear. What would the user need to do to invoke the control panel? How would we make this intuitive? Where would the control panel appear? We had many questions and issues to resolve.

We decided the control panel would have two states: a small informative state that contained the title of the icon the user was interacting with, and a fully expandable state if the user wanted to interact with the icon (such as rotating and viewing). First, let's cover when the control panel appears, and then we can dive into the more advanced functionality.

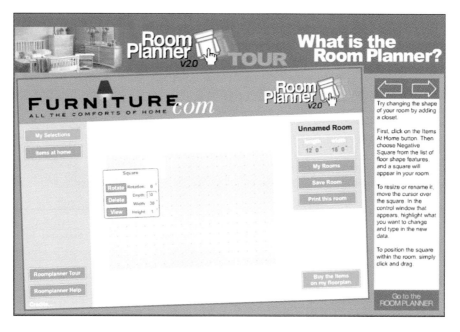

Figure 6.23 *Changing an item's depth with the control panel.*

We wanted the control panel to appear when the user rolls over the icon, but disappear when the user's intention is just to move or drag the icon. In the TILE Movie Clip frame labeled OVER, you'll see the following:

```
call ("/FLOOR/CP:come");
```

This tells the FLOOR Movie Clip (in which all the icons and the control panel exist) to call into the control panel and play the frame come, the code for which you see in Listing 6.3.

Listing 6.3   Code in the Frame Labeled come

```
 1: tileName = "/ROOM:tile" add tileNum;
 2: debug = tileName;
 3: itemName = eval(tileName add "_itemName");
 4: height = eval(tileName add "_height");
 5: width = eval(tileName add "_width");
 6: depth = eval(tileName add "_depth");
 7: rotation = eval(tileName add "_rotation");
 8: fetchPFID = eval(tileName add "_pfID");
 9: call ("setLocation");
10: if (Number(fetchPFID)>0) {
11:     setProperty ("dbleClick", _visible, true);
12: } else {
13:     setProperty ("dbleClick", _visible, false);
14: }
15: setProperty ("", _x, myX);
16: setProperty ("", _y, myY);
17: setProperty ("", _visible, true);
18: gotoAndStop ("Init");
```

All this scripting tells the control panel where to appear, what data to show, and whether or not to show the View button (dbleClick depending on whether it's a Furniture.com item or not). Let's quickly explain how.

Line 1 determines which tile we are working with and line 2 is a debug function for testing. (To keep it simple, just ignore line 2.) In line 3, we find the name of the item such as "Love Seat."

Lines 4–7 get the height, width, depth, and rotation value of the icon. Line 8 gets the Furniture.com item number; that is, its ID. In case the user wants to view it, we need to get this info from the database.

249

Line 9 calls to the setLocation frame, which sets the control panel's X and Y variables. The remaining lines set the position and visibility of the icon, and then sends Flash to the Init frame label.

It recognizes a Furniture.com item because it has a PFID number. It also decides whether or not the user can change the size. If it's a Furniture.com item, the user can't scale the item, but she can see the dimensions.

After many days of integrating these components and wiring everything together, we were very excited to see the piece functioning. However, we had one issue: If an icon were at the bottom of the screen or close to an edge, the control panel would appear partially outside the borders and become unusable.

The line call ("setLocation"); was integrated to handle this problem. The setLocation script to handle this is the following:

```
myX = getProperty ("/FLOOR/tile" add tileNum, _x);
myY = getProperty ("/FLOOR/tile" add tileNum, _y);
// If too far left, adjust x position
if (Number(myX)<Number(-120)) {
    myX = Number(myX)+133;
}
// If too low, adjust y position
if (Number(myY)>100) {
    myYAdjust = -100;
} else {
    myYAdjust = 0;
}
```

This ActionScripting checks whether the tile is low or left, and adjusts the variables so that the tile appears in the correct place. The first two lines determine where the icon is and line 3 is just some code commenting—which we should have done more of!

Lines 4–6 re-adjust the X position and value if the icon is too far left and the control panel won't be seen. Line 7 is more commenting, and line 8 does the same location testing for the Y value and position that was done earlier for the X value and position.

If the user wants to edit an icon or see the icon's details, the user rolls over the control panel, which calls to the frame named `full`. This then populates all the fields and blocks the dimensions if it's a Furniture.com item, and makes the View button invisible if it's not. This script is simple enough that if for some reason we were to increase the size of the control panel down the road, we could easily increase the buffer zone by adjusting the numbers and it would work.

Listing 6.4 shows the contents of the frame script `full` in the control panel.

Listing 6.4   The Script on the Frame Labeled full

```
 1: setProperty ("", _y, Number(myY)+Number(myYAdjust));
 2: nameBox:myText = itemName;
 3: if (Number(fetchPFID)>0) {
 4:     setProperty ("viewButtonMC", _visible, true);
 5:     setProperty ("blocker", _visible, true);
 6: } else {
 7:     setProperty ("viewButtonMC", _visible, false);
 8:     setProperty ("blocker", _visible, false);
 9: }
10: nameBox:returnValue1 = "/FLOOR/CP:itemName";
11: nameBox:returnValue2 = "/ROOM:tile" add tileNum add
➥"_itemName";
12: depthBox:myText = depth;
13: depthBox:returnValue1 = "/FLOOR/CP:depth";
14: depthBox:returnValue2 = "/ROOM:tile" add tileNum add
➥"_depth";
15: depthBox:min = /GLOBALS:MinTileDepth;
16: depthBox:max = /GLOBALS:MaxTileDepth;
17: depthBox:action = "/FLOOR/CP:update";
18: widthBox:myText = width;
```

251

Listing 6.4   Continued

```
19: widthBox:returnValue1 = "/FLOOR/CP:width";
20: widthBox:returnValue2 = "/ROOM:tile" add tileNum add
➥"_width";
21: widthBox:min = /GLOBALS:MinTileWidth;
22: widthBox:max = /GLOBALS:MaxTileWidth;
23: widthBox:action = "/FLOOR/CP:update";
24: heightBox:myText = height;
25: heightBox:returnValue1 = "/FLOOR/CP:height";
26: heightBox:returnValue2 = "/ROOM:tile" add tileNum
➥add "_height";
27: heightBox:min = 0;
28: heightBox:max = 999;
29: rotationBox:myText = rotation;
30: rotationBox:returnValue1 = "/FLOOR/CP:rotation";
31: rotationBox:returnValue2 = "/ROOM:tile" add tileNum
➥add "_rotation";
32: rotationBox:min = 0;
33: rotationBox:max = 360;
34: rotationBox:action = "/FLOOR/CP:update";
35: tellTarget ("/TileSound") {
36:     gotoAndStop ("slideOpen");
37: }
38: stop ();
```

The first line sets the position of the control panel so it appears over the correct icon. The second line outs the name of the item in the text field. Lines 3–9 determine whether the item is generic or Furniture.com's. If it is a Furniture.com item, it turns on the double-click functionality to view the item. If it's a Furniture.com item, lines 10 and 11 allow you to rename it, and then store this value in the Room and Floor Movie Clips so that it can be displayed as necessary.

Line 12 sets the depth value, and lines 13 and 14 store these values as we did with the icon name. Lines 15 and 16 put some restrictions on the maximum width and depth so that it stays controllable. Line 17 determines the state of the icon so that if the state changes from active to inactive, it changes accordingly.

Lines 18–34 perform the same functions listed earlier, but this time for width, height, and rotation. Finally, lines 35–37 tell the sound to play.

Now I'd like to walk you through rotating an icon. We decided that the Rotate button should be simple, so it rotates the items clockwise by 45-degree increments. By adjusting the number, we were able to easily explore different increments. In addition, users can enter the degree of rotation they would like into the rotation field in the control panel. Here's how it's done:

Listing 6.5   Rotating an Icon

```
 1: on (release) {
 2:     rotation = eval("/ROOM:tile" add tileNum add
"_rotation");
 3:     rotation = Number(rotation)+45;
 4:     if (Number(rotation)>360) {
 5:         rotation = 0;
 6:     }
 7:     setProperty ("/FLOOR/tile" add tileNum, _
➥rotation, rotation);
 8:     set ("/ROOM:tile" add tileNum add "_rotation",
➥rotation);
 9:     rotationBox:myText = rotation;
10: }
```

Lines 1 and 2 set the variable rotation to whatever the current rotated value of the icon is; after all, we have to start somewhere. Line 3 adds 45 degrees to the current rotation value because the user just clicked Rotate and we do so in 45-degree increments.

Lines 4–6 ensure that at 360 degrees, we start the degrees at 0 again. Line 7 actually rotates the icon by updating the rotation property. Line 8 stores the rotation value in ROOM for later retrieval and lines 9 and 10 update the rotation value displayed in the control panel.

Each item is kept track of within the ROOM movie clip. You can see that after we rotate the icon, we update the data of the icon in the ROOM. All the icon's attributes are kept track of in this way. This comes into play when you save, load, or buy a room. The Room Planner looks inside the ROOM and gathers all the data that's there. Every icon's position, scale, rotation, name, PFID (if applicable), and so on are captured.

Saving Rooms

We capture all this information so that users can come back at any time and have their room look the way they left it. It's rather necessary. I mean, imagine if your word processing program couldn't save, and you had to retype a letter every time you needed it—zoinks! Let's take this opportunity to discuss how we save room information.

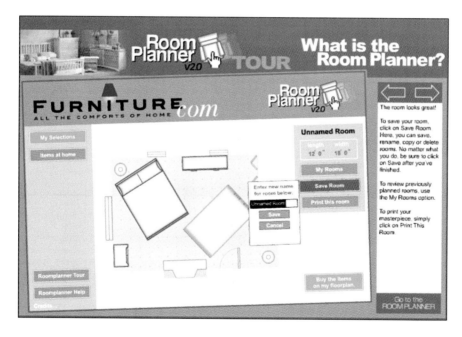

Figure 6.24   *That's a lovely room. Let's save it.*

Each registered user has a section of database with all her info stored there. The fetchRooms.asp page gets only the room names and stores them in the Rooms menu. As a user creates a new room, all the data for that room is stored in the ROOM Movie Clip, which contains no graphical information at all—just data and code. For example, when the user changes the dimensions of the floor, FLOOR updates ROOM with the new dimensions. When the user places an icon in her room, ROOM is told where the icon is and what it is. When the user moves that icon, ROOM is updated. You get the idea.

Every icon has a number associated with it and all its individual data is captured. Why store all this data here, you ask? Because when we want to save a room, we just tell ROOM to dump all its data to the saveRoom.asp. There is no other data in ROOM. In FLOOR or in the main movie, there might be other variables we are using for the functionality of the piece and we don't want to clutter or burden the data transfer. In reverse, when we want to load a room, we just clear all the data from ROOM and load all the new data in from loadRoom.asp into ROOM. Then we tell FLOOR to use that data to update itself.

Let's look at how simple this is in the saveRoom code found in the GLOBALS Movie Clip:

```
if (/GLOBALS:Registered) {
    DONE = false;
    loadVariables ("saveRoom.asp", "/ROOM", "POST");
} else {
    DONE = true;
    getURL ("registration.asp", "_self", "POST");
}
resume = "refresh";
gotoAndPlay ("WaitForDone");
```

Notice that the user must be registered to save. If the user is registered, the code just POSTs all variables from ROOM to saveRoom.asp. That's it, done deal. Let's start to wrap up our code review and talk about how to handle purchasing items from the Room Planner.

The `fetchGlobals.asp` passes in a registered variable to indicate to the Room Planner whether the user is registered or not. If the user is not registered, it doesn't run `saveRoom.asp` and instead opens the `registration.asp`, which prompts the user to register.

Buying Furniture

When a user decides he likes the layout and wants to purchase the items he has arranged so carefully in his room, he clicks the "Buy the items on my floorplan" button, which invokes the following code:

```
on (release) {
    call ("/ROOM:buyRoom");
}
```

In ROOM, we see the following for buyRoom:

Listing 6.6   Frame Script in buyRoom

```
1: purchase_list = "";
2: i = 0;
3: while (Number(i)<Number(/GLOBALS:MaxTiles)) {
4:     if (eval("tile" add i add "_used") and
➡(eval("tile" add i add "_pfID")>0)) {
5:         purchase_list = purchase_list add "," add
➡eval("tile" add i add "_pfID");
6:     }
7:     i = Number(i)+1;
8: }
9: purchase_list = substring(purchase_list, 2,
➡length(purchase_list)-1);
10: if (Number(length(purchase_list))>0) {
11:     call ("saveRoom");
12:     if (Number(/GLOBALS:PDC) == 1) {
13:         getURL ("/dcenter/purchase/purchase_1.asp",
                ➡"_self", "POST");
14:     } else {
```

Listing 6.6   Continued

```
15:        getURL ("/purchase/purchase_1.asp", "_self",
➥"POST");
16:     }
17: }
```

This creates a variable called `purchase_list` and then looks at all the data in ROOM. It checks each item to see whether there is a PFID number. If there is, it's a Furniture.com item and it is added to the list. After the list is created, the code calls `purchase_1.asp` and sends it the list, which will then be created into an order sheet. Bingo! Sale done! Let's quickly review this line by line.

Line 1 sets the variable `purchase list` to nothing in case the user clicked the buy button before and made purchases. Line 2 sets the index counter to 0. Line 3 keeps it looping until it reaches the number of tiles that the user has placed on the floor.

Line 4 examines each item to see whether it has a PFID. If one is found, it is added to the list. Line 7 indicates the end of the loop. Line 9 prepares the list of items for when the user decides to purchase.

Line 10 checks to make sure that it found something to be put in the list, and line 11 saves the room. Line 12 checks whether it is a user making a purchase or if it is a Furniture.com design rep making the purchase over the phone with the customer. Each uses a different purchase form, one for the customer and not the design rep. Line 15 posts the data to `purchase.asp` and goes to the purchase form. Whew.

Project Wrap-Up

About two weeks were spent coding the initial solution, and another two weeks integrating the Room Planner into the existing Furniture.com systems and databases. Surprisingly enough, very few issues came up in final QA. I remember just before the launch, we were presenting the nearly completed solution in one of the dining/conference rooms when Andrew Brooks, Furniture.com's CEO, walked in for a quick demonstration. I was all fired up to showcase our baby to the CEO. The presentation was brief but successful. Little did I know how important first impressions were; Andrew eventually offered me a job to come work for him at Furniture.com.

About a month after the launch, Furniture.com changed its logo, and we were forced to update the main file. After the company got a taste for improvements and realized how quickly we could handle them, the changes started rolling in. Ultimately, we spent nearly six months working on evolutions of the Room Planner, from adding functionality such as resizable floor sizes to minor interface enhancements.

The Flash community, including Macromedia, starting buzzing about the Room Planner and at its peak, I was receiving about three inquiries a week either to build or sell the Room Planner. We worked with Macromedia to develop a spotlight presentation that was showcased on the Macromedia Web site, and I was invited to speak at one of Macromedia'a Internet World presentations in New York.

Post-Mortem

In hindsight, the Room Planner was a phenomenal solution. I have yet to see a solution that has the same level of complexity and functionality, but that's probably just because I haven't looked hard enough. I wonder what the Room Planner would be like right now if we had been able to evolve it over this entire time?

It goes without saying that the client was extremely pleased. Statistics showed that users of the Room Planner stayed on the Web site for an average of one hour and

80% of all Room Planner users eventually bought product. This is an amazing return on investment.

We also learned that couples would collaborate using the Room Planner during the workday. One would log on in the morning, lay out a room the way they wanted, and log off. The other would then log in and make changes to the room as they saw fit. Hmmm, sounds like a good idea for the project we are working on right now.

We are excited that Generator has evolved as much as it has because now we can start to explore far more advanced solutions, such as the dynamic presentation and interaction of complex data. In addition, all the great Flash community members are constantly coming up with unique creations and products.

A few of these excellent people were a part of this project, from Misha's original vision to Yechezchal and Bill, who handled the original coding. Special praise should go to Phil Stephenson, who started on the team after the Room Planner launch, and was faced with the task of learning the ins and outs of the Room Planner on his own in order to support it when Bill and Yechezcahl moved on. That was quite a task, and I am happy to say that Phil and I are once again working together on other exciting new Flash projects, so hopefully you will hear from us again.

Just imagine what's possible with Generator, Swift3D, Swish, and all the new potential of Flash 5 ActionScripting with XML and the endless middleware technologies and software being developed daily combined with back-end datastores such as SQL, Oracle, and even Access!

Flash Resources on the Web

The number of Web sites that contain a significant amount of Flash-related information seems to be growing exponentially. Unfortunately, because of the speed of this growth, there's no way for a book (which goes to press some weeks before it appears in stores) to stay current. What I can do is give you a list of very worthwhile sites. Most of them will have made themselves even richer and more informative since I first encountered them. Some will have closed their doors and gone off in pursuit of other interests. One thing this list will do is help you make your own, much more up-to-date list because most of these sites have frequently updated links to other Flash sites.

Perhaps the most valuable aspect of many of these sites is that they contain Flash ActionScript and JavaScript code that you are invited to download and modify for your own use. Some of these sites have so many FLAs and tutorials that there's not room to describe them in any depth.

About.Com

http://webdesign.miningco.com/compute/webdesign/
msubflash.htm

About.com is a Web resource for all sorts of information about the Web, including Flash. Much of that information is links to other sites on the list, but they are listed according to the topics they cover. This makes it an excellent way to find quick solutions to problems—especially those that are related to Flash but that also involve other Web technologies.

Accueil Flash

http://perso.wanadoo.fr/phol/flash/index.htm

This is a French site with numerous downloadable Flash 4 movie files.

Art's Website

http://www.artswebsite.com/coolstuff/flash.htmArt's Website features a good many Flash tutorials.

BertoFlash

http://www.bertoflash.nu

BertoFlash is a French site that has quite a few examples online. When I visited, the site was partially in English and partially in French; a notice was posted that an English version of the entire site would be available soon. There were quite a few routines on this site, neatly divided into categories: Flash/JavaScript, ASP/Perl, Flash 4, and Flash 5. You can play the sample movies onscreen, but you cannot download them. You can, however, request the FLA files, and they will be sent to you by e-mail.

Canfield Studios—Flash 3 Samples

`http://www.canfieldstudios.com/flash3`

Canfield has a large number of Flash 3 and Flash 4 sample files that you can play on the Web. Almost all of them let you download the source file as well. However, there is a request that you not download the source files and then claim them as your own. There's also a long list of additional Flash links.

No Flash 5 files had been posted when I last looked.

FlashFilmMaker.com

`http://www.flashfilmmaker.com/`

This site includes lessons, articles, a community forum, and a talent directory.

Cleopatra Art Group

`http://move.to/cleoag`

This site features Flash tips, tricks, and source files.

Code 66

`http://www.code66.com/demo/flash/`

This site includes FLA files and tutorials.

Designs by Mark

`http://www.designsbymark.com/flashtut/`

This site carries a variety of tutorials on Flash, Photoshop, Illustrator, and general Web design.

Extreme Flash

http://www.extremeflash.com/

Lots of FLAs and tutorials that are up-to-date for Flash 4 and 5 appear on this site.

Fay Studios

http://www.webpagetogo.com/FS/WD/

Fay's site features basic tutorials on using Flash.

The Flash Academy

http://www.enetserve.com/tutorials/

This is presented by ENS Inc. and Flasher.net. As one would guess from its name, this site features quite a list of tutorials, source files, and templates.

Flash.com

http://www.flash.com/

The Macromedia Flash page has lots of links to other Flash resources. Those links are constantly being updated and revised. There are also many examples of outstanding Flash sites and applications, and online forums that are an excellent place to get and share tips, tricks, and information, including getting ratings of your site. Macromedia has also added the Flash Exchange, where users can upload and download extensions for Flash. This is an excellent place to start if you just want to see what Flash can do or need a little inspiration.

Flahoo.com

http://www.flahoo.com

A directory of cool Flash sites, Flahoo.com does not have any downloadables.

Flashmove

http://www.flashmove.com

There are lots of downloadable source files on this site. The
FLAs are especially oriented toward game builders, but that
doesn't mean business developers won't find anything
useful here.

FlashPlanet

http://www.flashplanet.com/

This is an excellent site that includes quite a few tutorials
with the Flash files: Flipping pages, Draggable window with
close button, Full Flash site, and 3D talking head animation.
There are also quite a few sounds and clip art files.

FlashBible

http://www.flashbible.com/

There is a worthwhile list of FLAs at the FlashBible site.

FlashKit

http://www.flashkit.com/

A Flash resource site presented in HTML, FlashKit has many
different categories of information, including tutorials and
message boards.

FlashLite

http://www.flashlite.net

Another rich site for the advanced ActionScripter is
FlashLite.

Flash Jester

http://www.flashjester.com

This site features third-party Flash tools, including screensaver creation tools. Just think—you can put your company site on all your employees' screens.

Flash Magazine

http://www.flashmagazine.com/flash4.htm

This online magazine about Flash has a pretty good rundown of all the Flash 5 features.

FlashMaster

http://www.flashmaster.nu

This site features tutorials, source FLAs, and message boards.

Flash Pro

http://www.flashpro.nl/

This is a fairly new Dutch site that's all in English. You can take tutorials and upload FLAs for deconstruction.

Flazoom

http://www.Flazoom.com

Flazoom is probably best described as a Flash magazine. There are articles on solving problems in Flash. Also, there are links to sites that the editors feel might be particularly helpful or inspirational. Not much here in the way of sample FLA files the last time I checked.

Flashwave

http://www.egomedia.freeserve.co.uk/index2.html

Flashwave is an online magazine and Flash resource, primarily aimed at advanced users and programmers.

Tutorials include mouse tracking, ASP database connection advanced tutorials, chat tutorial, and connecting to CGI to read random strings.

HelpCentre

http://www.helpcentre.co.uk

This threaded messaging board is dedicated to discussions about various aspects of Flash.

i/US Flash Conference

http://www.i-us.com/macromed.htm

This site hosts Macromedia conferences on each of the major Macromedia products. Conference topics are listed by subject.

Macromedia Flash Support Center

http://www.macromedia.com/support/flash/

This is the Flash support section of the Macromedia Web site. In addition to Macromedia University, which offers Flash lessons for pay, there are very helpful discussions centering on the topics of most concern to Flash developers. Although this isn't the only worthwhile authority on Flash techniques, it is certainly one of the first places you should look.

Mano1

http://www.mano1.com

Yet another Flash guru's site, Mano1 has been redesigned, and the results are impressive. The main interface is a list of links to Mano1 sites.

Moock WebDesign Flash

http://www.moock.org/webdesign/flash/index.html

Moock has lots of helpful tutorials on Flash 4 techniques. Most will stand you in good stead, except that the language has changed. There's an especially long session on ActionScript and another on JavaScript. Also very worthwhile is a list of bugs in Internet Explorer for the Mac.

Nuthing but Flash

http://nuthing.com

Nik Kihnani's site demonstrates a few animation techniques that are especially suited to the scientifically minded. The main animation is living proof of the effectiveness of repeating symbols as a method of making complex designs.

Phresh

http://www.phresh.de

Phresh is a Flash Web zine that features current news about late-breaking Flash developments. It is especially on top of third-party products that do something to make Flash easier or faster or both. There are also related tutorials on such subjects as ASP coding, and there's an ActionScript guide (not yet updated to accommodate Flash 5).

PS Woods Flash Yin and Yang

```
http://www.wdvl.com/Multimedia/Flash/Yin-n-Yang/
```

This site is a tutorial on building a somewhat advanced
Web site.

Quintus Flash Index

```
http://quintus.org
```

Quintus offers 1,000 links to other Flash resources.

Flashgeek.com

```
http://www.flashgeek.com
```

Flashgeek showcases Rick Turoczy's tutorials on techniques
for integrating Flash and PowerPoint. You'll be surprised at
what a cool and powerful combination this can be. In fact,
you'll probably get all sorts of ideas.

ShockFusion

```
http://www.shockfusion.com
```

ShockFusion bills itself as "a free resource for Flash
developers worldwide." The site for the FlashForward 2000
conferences, ShockFusion also provides a serious amount of
content for Flash developers of all stripes. There are links to
award-winning cool sites, cartoons, and games; a section on
solving design problems in Flash; a Flash jobs bulletin
board; a session on audio techniques; and a discussion on
Flash 5.

Trainingtools.com

```
http://www.trainingtools.com
```

This is a site that offers several online courses on popular
graphics and programming topics, including Flash 5, Flash 4

scripting, and Flash 4. There are also courses on related technologies, such as Dreamweaver, JavaScript, and Photoshop.

Virtual-FX

`http://www.virtual-fx.net`

This site features excellent ActionScript tutorials. For instance, the search engine tutorial is very carefully commented, making it much easier to modify than most. The site is extremely rich in both tutorial and open-source FLA content. There were, when I last checked, 177 tutorials and 78 open source files.

Webmonkey: Multimedia Collection

`http://www.hotwired.com/webmonkey/multimedia/
?tw=frontdoor`

Wired magazine's Web developer's resource, Webmonkey contains Flash tutorials.

Were-Here

`http://www.were-here.com/forum/ultimate.html`

One of the most highly respected Flash reference sites, Were-Here has a table of contents that would take up a good part of this book's reference section. There are 85 tutorials, including several on Flash 5, and 330 downloadable open-source FLAs in the following categories: 3D, ActionScript code, Animation and Effects, Games, Generator, JavaScript, Math Functions, Menus and Navigation, Mouse Trails, Site Structure, SmartClips, Sound and Music, Text Effects, Utilities, Widgets, Flash 5 Menus, and a half-dozen or so new Flash 5 routines.

zinc roe Design

`http://www.zincroe.com/flash/`

This show-off site for Jason Krogh features 17 "semi" open-source FLA files (you're welcome to use them, as long as it's not for commercial purposes).

Flash Mailing Lists

flasher-l

`http://www.chinwag.com/flasher`

An unmoderated discussion forum for developers using Macromedia Flash.

Flashpro

`http://www.muinar.com/flashpro`

A mailing list for professional Macromedia Flash developers.

pro_flash

`http://www.onelist.com/subscribe.cgi/pro_flash`

Dedicated to professional Macromedia Flash developers. Just go to the Web site to sign up.

FSDesigners

`http://www.egroups.com/group/FSdesigners`

Macromedia Flash design.

Flash-Related Software

Macromedia Generator

http://www.macromedia.com/software/generator/

The Generator enables delivery of dynamic graphic content. In other words, what the viewer sees depends on his interaction with buttons and forms on the site. There are two versions of the program, the Developer Edition (primarily for developers building prototypes) and the Enterprise Edition (the high-volume, high-performance, high-price version). Both editions have two components: authoring templates for Flash and server software.

Flash Writer

http://www.macromedia.com/software/flash/download/flashwriter/

This plug-in for Adobe Illustrator lets it directly export Flash files.

Swift 3D

http://www.swift3d.com/

Swift 3D is a 3D program made by Electric Rain (http://www.erain.com/) that writes animated 3D Flash files.

Vectra 3D

http://www.vecta3d.com/

Vectra 3D can be obtained either as a plug-in for 3D Studio Max or as a standalone application for both Mac and Windows. The standalone will accept .DXF 3D models built in most anything. You can also extrude 2D Flash images into 3D, and then animate the 3D and export the animation as Flash.

Kimmuli.com

http://www.kimmuli.com/#

Kimmuli is a visual help tool for Generator; Bohdi is for making Generator COM objects for ASP, and Quassia is a Dreamweaver plug-in for Flash that lets you get rid of the default cursor so that you can simulate your own for drag-and-drop animations.

Swish

http://swishzone.com

Swish produces automated text effects for Macromedia Flash.

OpenSWF

http://www.openswf.org

OpenSWF specializes in .swf file formatting.

Swifty Utilities

http://buraks.com/swifty

Swifty develops tools for opening and organizing .swf files and elements.

OpenSWF

http://www.openswf.org

A collection of tools for extending Macromedia Flash.

3D Software

Dimensions

http://www.adobe.com/support/downloads/main.html

Dimensions extrudes 3D from 2D vector files (especially fonts). It is capable of output to Adobe Illustrator format, so the vector files can be imported directly into Flash, eliminating the need to trace over a bitmap.

Rhino3D

http://www.rhino3d.com

A full-featured, modeling program for less than $800, Rhino3D lets you import 3D models from 3D Studio Max and then export them as vector outlines that can be directly imported into Flash. All coloring has to be added inside Flash. This is Windows-only software, but it will run on Macs with Virtual PC.

Xara 3D

http://www.xara.com

An inexpensive program, Xara 3D lets you convert any type of text to 3D and animate it.

MetaStream

http://www.metastream.com

A program for creating 3D demos for the Web, MetaStream is an ideal solution for e-commerce sites that need to allow viewers to see a product from all sides. It could have important application in training and demo sites as well.

Blender

http://www.blender.nl

Blender is a very powerful 3D program that runs on numerous operating systems (but not any version of the Mac OS). Mac owners can run it under Linux. This program is shareware, but purchase of a (very affordable) key can unlock the latest and most powerful features.

Other Software

Flash 4 Database

http://www.kessels.com/flashdb/

This is a freeware program for storing and serving data from a database to Flash 4+.

Streamline

www.adobe.com

Streamline is the ideal program for converting bitmapped sketches to editable vector graphics that can be imported into Flash. Streamline gives you considerably more control over how the image is converted into a drawing than if you use the built-in, auto-trace capabilities present in most other illustration programs.

Font Software

TTCoverter

http://www6.zdnet.com/cgi-bin/texis/swlib/mac/
infomac.html?fcode=MC13911

This shareware converts Windows TrueType fonts to Mac TT fonts.

Music Resources

Flash Sounds

http://www.sounds.muinar.com/

All these sounds are specifically designed for Flash.

License Music

http://www.licensemusic.com/

Large collection of licensed music, including familiar titles.

Music4Flash

http://www.music4flash.com/

Good collection of royalty-free and inexpensive loops.

INDEX

M

283

X-Z

Other Related Titles